The Unsentimental Journey
of Laurence Sterne

The Unsentimental Journey
of Laurence Sterne

ERNEST NEVIN DILWORTH

1969

OCTAGON BOOKS

New York

Reprinted 1969

by special arrangement with Ernest Nevin Dilworth

OCTAGON BOOKS

A DIVISION OF FARRAR, STRAUS & GIROUX, INC.

19 Union Square West

New York, N. Y. 10003

LIBRARY OF CONGRESS CATALOG CARD NUMBER: 75-75990

Printed in U.S.A. by
TAYLOR PUBLISHING COMPANY
DALLAS, TEXAS

DEDICATION

L——d! said my mother—

Note

I SEND special thanks for their tolerance and kindliness to Professors Marjorie Hope Nicolson, Ernest Hunter Wright, and James Lowry Clifford, all of Columbia University. Permission to quote from the biographically invaluable *Letters of Laurence Sterne*, edited by Lewis Perry Curtis, has been generously granted by Mr. Curtis and the Clarendon Press. My sister Mrs. Maurice Johnson volunteered to type the hideous manuscript. I have been flattering my sisters for years.

Contents

Foreword

I F WE WERE TO READ NO STERNE, but only commentaries on him, I
think we should come to a two-fold conclusion: that he is a
great comic artist and also our Master Sniveller. Then, in thinking
over what we had read about the snivelling, we should begin to be
confused; for the commentators are not in agreement on the nature of his sentimentality. They find his sentiment in one way or
another tending always to excess, but they do not agree as to
whether it is honest to begin with. Is Sterne's sentiment sincere
or is it affected? That, as we pondered, would seem to be the question on which they first diverge. As we went on to read more commentaries, even the idea that Sterne is sentimental would begin to
divide into questionable shapes to plague us: Is his sentiment only
virtuosity, or is it satire, perhaps, or shameless fun? If our habit
of reading books about books was strong, we might even wish, in
our bewilderment, that someone would make a study of just this
matter of sentiment in Sterne—one that, somewhat methodically,
should call attention to Sterne's encounters with the feelings;
should consider them critically in their context; and should clarify
both their nature and the artist's intent. That is the sort of book I
have tried to write. Really, I mean to encourage the reading of
Sterne himself; and I have put into this book as much of him as
was feasible. Such relevant passages as I neither quote nor refer
to are, I hope, covered by my treatment of similar ones.

But the reader—particularly if he has not read the commentaries

—may want some proof that there is any problem here worth bothering about.

First of all, Sterne's chief subject matter is sentiment. We should suppose, since he does know how to write, that he should be able to make himself clear. Yet listen to the extremes of criticism on *A Sentimental Journey*.

> We laugh, cry, sneer, sympathise by turns. We change from one emotion to its opposite in the twinkling of an eye. This light attachment to the accepted reality, this neglect of the orderly sequence of narrative, allows Sterne almost the license of a poet. . . .
>
> If Sterne distresses us, it is for another reason. And here the blame rests partly at least upon the public—the public which had been shocked, which had cried out after the publication of *Tristram Shandy* that the writer was a cynic who deserved to be unfrocked. Sterne, unfortunately, thought it necessary to reply.
>
> "The world has imagined [he told Lord Shelburne] because I wrote *Tristram Shandy*, that I was myself more Shandean than I really ever was. . . . If it [*A Sentimental Journey*] is not thought a chaste book, mercy on them that read it, for they must have warm imaginations, indeed!"
>
> Thus in *A Sentimental Journey* we are never allowed to forget that Sterne is above all things sensitive, sympathetic, humane; that above all things he prizes the decencies, the simplicities of the human heart. And directly a writer sets out to prove himself this or that our suspicions are aroused. For the little extra stress he lays on the quality he desires us to see in him, coarsens it and over-paints it, so that instead of humour, we get farce, and instead of sentiment, sentimentality. Here, instead of being convinced of the tenderness of Sterne's heart—which in *Tristram Shandy* was never in question—we begin to doubt it. For we feel that Sterne is thinking not of the thing itself but of its effect upon our opinion of him. . . . Indeed, the chief fault of *A Sentimental Journey* comes from Sterne's concern for our good opinion of his heart.

That is Virginia Woolf in her introduction to the World's Classics edition of the book. The *Critical Review*, in 1768, had a different opinion:

> The author hired a post-chaise, and set out in a delirium, which appears never to have left him to the end of his journey; a fatal symptom of his approaching dissolution. It had, however, the temporary happy effect of making the sufferings of others the objects of his mirth, and not only rendering him insensible to the feelings of humanity, but superior to every regard for taste, truth, observation, or reflection.

What kind of journey has Sterne actually made? Does he pretend to a delicate sensibility or does he callously flout the feelings? Neither, we infer when Mr. Wilbur Cross, in his *Life and Times of Laurence Sterne*, says that the *Journal to Eliza* (known for its lunatic sentimentality) "completely reveals the pathological state of the emotions—long suspected but never quite known to a certainty—whence sprang the *Sentimental Journey*." And Coleridge, in *Table Talk*, had called the latter book "poor sickly stuff." On the other hand, Sterne's friend John Hall-Stevenson, the man who knew him best, seems, by his crude continuation of the *Journey*, to have agreed with the *Critical Review* as to what Sterne was doing. Imitating in clodhopper fashion the master's technical tricks, Hall-Stevenson rudely tramples those flowers of Sensibility over which, as some might say, the toes of Sterne had passed with a teasing grace.[1]

This at least is not unanimity.

Until his death Sterne, though celebrated for his skill in pathos, was always being compared with Rabelais, and one finds such imitations of him as a "Shandean Essay on Human Passions; with a Smack here and there of Butler, Prior, Swift, Pope, &c. By Caleb McWhim." As the nineteenth century draws near, there is a shift of interest; we have begun to lose that taste for wit and satire which had savoured, even in tears, their dash of salt. We become preoccupied with the feelings; we never toy any more except in earnest. For these or other reasons including, no doubt, the tendency of men to follow one another's lead, criticism in the nineteenth and twentieth centuries nods briefly at the humor in Sterne and then sidles up to the sentiment. Infrequently, for a moment at a time, criticism seems to have found this sentiment to be only an illusion—as when Mr. Cross says that Sterne "was a humorist pure and simple, and nothing else"; or when Mr. Rufus Putney, while wondering how much of Sterne's sentiment was real,[2] suggests that the *Journey* was a hoax by which Sterne satisfied at once his sense of humor and a need he felt to please the public with the pathos they wanted. And there is Carl August Behmer,[3] who says that Sterne parodied the faults of Richardson, of Locke, and of the English character, but goes on to find his "idealistic humor" full of feeling. Here once more pop up the questions whether Sterne's sentiment is satire, virtuosity, or fun. They appear in an untoward season.

Apart from these few brief protestations, there seems to be little doubt of Sterne's sentimentality. In the *Quarterly Review* in 1854, the Rev. Whitwell Elwin speaks for the critical public at large:

> The "Sentimental Journey" has some beautiful passages which are familiar to everybody, but a capital defect pervades the whole, which is embodied in the fact that it has brought the word *sentimental* into discredit, and made it the standard epithet for feelings that are sickly and superficial. The elaborate effort to work up every scene for effect is painfully visible, and, in spite of touches of genuine pathos, the general impression left by the book is that it is affected, morbid, and hollow. . . . Many of the incidents may be suspected to be fictitious.

What we want to know is whether it is good sentimentality or bad sentimentality, sincere or affected, natural or trumped-up. Thackeray, however, is almost alone in stating the question, and even he has half an answer.

> How much was deliberate calculation and imposture—how much was false sensibility—and how much true feeling? Where did the lie begin, and did he know where? and where did the truth end in the art and scheme of this man of genius, this actor, this quack? . . . He used to blubber perpetually in his study, and finding his tears infectious, and that they brought him a great popularity, he exercised the lucrative gift of weeping: he utilized it, and cried on every occasion.

In the *Dictionary of National Biography* is the downright reply of Sidney Lee.

> Sterne's reasoning faculty was incapable of controlling his constitutional sensitiveness to pain and pleasure. . . . The indelicate innuendoes which he foists on sedate words and situations, and the tears that he represented himself as shedding over dead asses and caged starlings, had an equally spontaneous origin in what was in him the normal state of his nerves.

Unlike Lee, Mr. E. A. Baker, in his *History of the English Novel*, sees the sentiment as anything but spontaneous:

> Sincerity, in the thing written if not in the writer, is a primary requirement in literature, of whatever kind. Anything false, affected, overcharged, or merely equivocal, excites suspicion, misses the mark, fails to impress in the way intended. Sterne's too often strikes the ordinary cold-blooded reader as false sentiment; he appears to be constantly working himself up into the required mood, forcing the tears to come; and, since he thoroughly enjoyed a weep, no doubt that is just what he is doing.

Mr. Cross, on the other hand, speaks in defense of Sterne's sincerity: "Exceedingly sensitive to pleasure and to pain, he gave way to the emotions of the moment, receiving no guidance from reason, for he had none." But according to Mr. George Sampson's *Concise Cambridge History of English Literature*, "The pathos of Dickens is naturally poured out; the pathos of Sterne is unnaturally put on." This we can to some degree match with what M. Cazamian (to whom the *Letters to Eliza* are "full of the most romantic fire") says in his *History of English Literature:*

> Psychological duality is the characteristic feature of an attitude, such as that of Sterne; and consciousness or artifice does not exclude with him the sincerity of emotion.

Insincerity is the more frequent charge. Sometimes it is made with a moral emphasis, as in Edmund Gosse's *History of Eighteenth Century Literature*—

> It has to be added . . . that his sentimentality is commonly only skin deep, and adopted more for purposes of intellectual self-indulgence than for philanthropy.

—and sometimes with an aesthetic one, as by H. D. Traill and Leslie Stephen, whose pleasure is spoiled by the inartistic and unnatural sudden starts and stops of the fountain of tears, and by the intrusion of the artist into his story, handkerchief in hand, bidding us indulge with him the luxury of weeping.

Perhaps the ultimate compromise—the conclusion that in Sterne sentimentality was married to self-control—is provided by Francis Bickley in his introduction to the Abbey Classics edition of *A Sentimental Journey*.

> Sentimentality, as Sterne understood, felt, and practised it, is an abnormal sensitiveness and reaction to emotional stimuli. The other consumptives, aware of their sensitiveness and frightened of it, have resisted their reactions, or at any rate denied them in their art. Sterne, on the other hand, not only accepted them but cultivated them and turned them into literary capital. He went out of his way to encounter stimuli against which to react. He could not live without frequent recourse to the drug of feeling. . . .
>
> The truth is that Sterne was saved, from the literary point of view, by an intellect which was stronger than his body or his nerves. He lost his heart a hundred times, but he never lost his head. Even while he suffered from his hyperaesthesia, he could watch its processes, detached and smiling.

Yet the question continues to rise out of Sterneian biography, editing, and criticism: What is the nature of the sentiment in Sterne? Is it excessive—is it sentimentality, in other words—because he could not help himself, or because he consciously indulged his sensibility, or because he wished to lay claim to feelings that he did not have? Or is the sentiment itself a jest? The answer must lie, if anywhere, in the words of Sterne, grinning at us like his picture, over all the years.

But so much for the background to our tale.

[xiv]

1

A Preface on Conclusions

THE PUBLIC CANNOT BEAR A JESTER. Not that people find it pain-ful to laugh—the jokes of Uncle John and the latest profes-sional comedian, and that incident on the doorstep after break-fast, are among the treasures of daily living; but our amusement springs out of custom; it is a flower of society; and laughter itself trembles in a moment of time at the edge of a cliff that has a name. Laughter is our guest and it had better behave itself; it must appear to conform to our principles and pull a long face at the right moments. Because, on the whole, human life is not very funny to man, the sense of humor is a mere firefly light, feeble and flicker-ing at best, and condemned to sleep for a season at a time. We take a good deal of trouble to live (though we are willing to die for a grave proposition), and by means of convictions we find our north, and learn to shelter ourselves from the wild beasts of the night and the cosmic weather. If only to keep from being flung off the planet, we say, each man must discover for himself the law of gravity. And so the jester is conceivable only against a background of pathos; if, true to his jest, he whips that background away, the public is left facing the abyss and a suspended grin that can only be that of a devil.

One of the victims of our rigid and fearful simplicity is Laurence Sterne, once famous as the author of two books that once were read. He called himself Yorick, and was a lightfoot wit inordinately fond of double meanings, who made the word *sentimental* popular all over the world. Why *sentimental?* What has a king's jester to do with the cult of tender hearts and facile tears? It is by a coinci-

[1]

dence of time that we have had a jester (smiling through his tears, like all clowns that we can safely imagine) who, finding lachrymosity lying in his way, took it for a considerable part of his subject matter.

I first learned the meaning of *sentimental* in the nineteen-twenties, a holiday time in which the word was much used and always with contempt. It was then that I first read *Tristram Shandy* and was first told that such and such passages in it are sentimental and that the author himself was a sentimentalist. Though perhaps not the dullest child in school at that time, I was not quite able to understand what, in their pious repetition of previous judgments, my teachers were talking about. "Uncle Toby and the Fly—" they would explain. Having learned to bow to authority, I made my bow, forgot the matter, and went on enjoying Sterne in my desultory way.

I think I understand them now.

Sterne has had a sad posthumous history. Not only has he had to pass through the sieve of human needs and human revulsions, but he has been shaken and scattered by the mere priggishness and prudery and ignorance of the times. Known at first as a humorist, a little later as a humorist with much skill in the manipulation of pathos, he was hoisted soon after his death (and chiefly by Germans, Frenchmen, and others who could not read English) into a throne as the prince of sentimentalists; since then he has been outlawed from all but one of the conventional heavens as an ineffectually maudlin posturer and a low fellow. There have been a few attempts to apologise for him, to make our hearts bleed for a victim of frustration, to explain what has often been called the Mystery of his Personality; but the critical majority have triumphed, and a thousand textbooks echo the inconclusive cadences that have set him down as an eccentric and indecent humorist, a famous tear-jerker (though not an entirely satisfactory one), an immoral parson and, O yes, a great writer and one of the fathers of the English novel. The vagueness of all this as literary criticism bothers practically nobody. After all, when the essence of a man's work has gone to heaven in a textbook, there is as little necessity to think about that work as to dig it up and read it. The society of students

[2]

and teachers, in its aversion to the critical process, simply reflects that larger and enveloping society which would rather die than examine the catchwords with which it poisons itself.

It may be that a reasonably serious examination of sentimentality in Sterne might, in dispelling an inherited bogey, not only encourage a few timid sophisticates to read the man, but also restore to him enough literary integrity to make his work believable.

What it is to be sentimental in these days everybody knows. I have every intention of not ballooning about in the philosophical upper air; the abstracted paradoxes of extended meanings have no place in an essay of this sort, whose life depends on a polite sobriety. And so sentimentality will be excessive emotion, the waste of feeling on what are called trivial and unworthy objects, and the indulgence of emotion apparently for its own sake. We may agree to take it for granted that however ridiculous or revolting, however facile or cheap or tawdry the sentimental may be, the sentimental person is in earnest; he is feeling the thing. The odor of affectation that has come to cling to the sentimental is an inference of the outsider, and the impression of falsity is a decision in human values. Custom may decide how many tears and sighs are to be allotted to what objects and on what occasions, but either feeling is genuine or it is not felt. And the man who pretends to weep is not only being sociable, he is playing with the human heart.

Obviously there could have been no such thing as an eighteenth-century cult of sensibility without the help of considerable good-natured cynicism. People do not feel symphonically. On the other hand, a fashion owes as much to the spirit of the times as it does to deliberation. Sentimentalism, fully established in France and England long before Sterne began to write, was a literary evidence that people were tired of the old tyrants; the heart, after all, had its reasons, and it was time for the world to take off its superhuman armor and become a bit gentler, more intimate and accommodating.* This it did, as the material remains of those days most gra-

* It is customary at this juncture to mention Shaftesbury, who invented the Moral Sense, and Hutcheson who, so late as the eighteenth century, thought of making benevolence a virtue. The study of influences is an amusing game, for everything that exists is a derivation. These men undoubtedly were read; so were Latitudinarian divines, and Pascal and platonic romancers; Protestantism

ciously tell us. But that everyone who wrote in praise of natural goodness, and cultivated the humane impulse, and promoted the flow of tears, and amplified the beating of the heart—that every such person was moved by genuine feeling, it is unnecessary to believe. We have had a similar fashion in our own day, when the writer who forgot to concern himself with our social problems, and take the part of the unfortunate, was called a bad man. We have our own clichés that anoint us virtuous; so had the eighteenth century. And when Sterne first encountered the figure of Sensibility, she was draped in conventional robes; emotionalism and its appurtenances were already stylised. The clothing had long been at hand; and the melodious tear which Milton ceremoniously ordered for Lycidas was simply put into mass-production.

The machine was geared for sympathy and soul. Swift, Hogarth, Fielding, Smollett, Sterne, remind us of human fact; push them aside and see how the more popular artists float their age off on honey-dripping clouds. Exquisite little feet kiss the absent-minded paths they travel; the sharp corners of the world are remodeled in compassionate, melting curves; pleasing sorrows chime in shared, sublimated harmonies; buttocks, quite disembodied, bless fragile chairs. How do they get that way? Humanity abhors a fact, and has been snubbing its own flesh for thousands of years. The heart, as a symbol, is always in danger of being confused with the soul. When the market-price of the heart went up, the heart left the body behind; the feelings became valuable in themselves, were over-refined and over-elevated; and man's vaguest inner promptings found themselves dressed to the nines and provided with a coach, a town house, and a place in the country. Today we have vagueness enthroned; compassion is a thing of the past.

At the peak of fashion, *sensibility* needed an adjective that, unlike *sensible*, would stick to the point. The word *sentimental* took over the work of describing what was distinguished by fine feeling, by sympathy and benevolence, by a spiritual rather than a bodily tenderness. Its fortunes were those of the faddists who employed it. "What," asked someone five years before Sterne's first

---

and Rebellion and the rise of the homely middle classes came before them, and men found virtue in sympathetic chairs and gardens without their guidance.

book was published—"what can be more nobly human than to have a tender sentimental feeling of our own and others' misfortunes?" * Before it retired from the stage to its present seat of disgrace, the word had made every decent emotion a part of its repertory. Here are some book-titles.

Sentimental Fables. Designed chiefly for the Use of Ladies. 1772. The intention of the author was to "inculcate the most liberal and exalted sentiments . . . to affect the heart by strongly exciting the *passions*, and to gain over the judgement by connecting them with their proper objects."
Sentimental Discourses upon Religion and Morality. By a Lady. 1776.
The Sentimental Spouter: or young actor's companion &c. &c. The whole comprising the essence of theatrical delivery and the beauties of dramatic poetry. 1774. (I have not seen this, but dare say it was serious. In Enfield's *Speaker* the St. Crispian speech is to be found under "Pathetic Pieces.")

The disgrace was gradual. Constant ridicule by the humorists had no effect; eighteenth-century sentimentalism played itself out. When two of its most successful exploiters turned upon it, the jig was up. Sensibility had overreached itself, the word *sentimental* had lost face, and sentimentality hid behind a beard. In 1786, nearly twenty years after the death of Sterne, we find Richard Cumberland satirising his own milch cow.

Retirement is a charming subject for a sentimental enthusiast. There is not a poet in the language, but will help him out

* From a letter in *Man*, No. 43, October 22, 1755. For *sensibility* in full flower we have this early definition: "Humanity, in its first and general Acceptation, is call'd by Holy Writers, *Good-will towards Men*; by Heathens, *Philanthropy*, or *Love* of our *Fellow Creatures*. It sometimes takes the Name of *Good-nature*, and *delights* in Actions that have an *obliging* Tendency in them: When strongly *impress'd* on the *Mind*, it assumes a *higher* and nobler Character, and is not satisfy'd with *good-natured* Actions alone, but *feels* the *Misery* of others with *inward Pain*. It is then deservedly named *Sensibility*, and is considerably increased in its intrinsick Worth. . . ."—*Prompter*, No. 63, June 17, 1735. I owe these lexicographical illustrations to R. S. Crane: "Suggestions Toward a Genealogy of the 'Man of Feeling,' " *Journal of English Literary History*, I, 3 (Dec. 1934), 205–230.

with a description; Musidorus had them all at his fingers ends, from *Hesperus that led the starry host,* down to a glow-worm. . . .

"Oh! horrible!" cried Sappho, interrupting him, "I will never marry; I will never so contaminate the spotless lustre of my incorporeal purity." [1]

And the cool Mackenzie, the Man of Feeling himself, treating of the species of sentimental novels, says,

> That creation of refined and subtile feeling, reared by the authors of the works to which I allude, has an ill effect, not only on our ideas of virtue, but also on our estimate of happiness. That sickly sort of refinement creates imaginary evils and distresses, and imaginary blessings and enjoyments, which embitter the common disappointments, and depreciate the common attainments, of life. [2]

A diagnosis that has its twentieth-century applications.

On the whole, the age was as sane as any other. From beginning to end of it there were voices saying, in a hundred accents, that the good man, the ideal human being, is one who tempers reason with sensibility, sensibility with reason—and so long as a man is pictured as his own musical instrument, the doctrine makes sense. It happened that intemperate sensibility made a loud, though cultured, noise. It also happened that there were humorists in the neighborhood. Sterne was one of them.

If Sterne did not invent the word *sentimental* [3] he at least immortalised it. He wrote it out freely but not wastefully, and with the following discoverable meanings:

> Characterised by platonically pure, tender, and delicious sentiments—between the sexes—as in certain parts of the "best French romances."
>
> Involving a sympathetic "vibration in the strings, about the region of the heart."
>
> Distinguished by fine, delicate, or elevated feelings.
>
> Philosophically gallant.
>
> Demanding spiritual rather than physical satisfaction.

[6]

Heartfelt.
Lovesick.
Commemorative of a Grand Passion.
Affecting.

It is a convenient adjective for the nouns *sentiment, sensibility,* and *sensation* (feeling), and a synonym for *good-hearted, humane,* and *generous*. A useful word, in fact—and before the man of science draws up a chair beside us, he should be presented with something in the nature of a comment, from a letter Sterne wrote to John Wodehouse in 1765.

> I carry on my affairs quite in the French way, sentimentally —*"L'amour"* (say they) *"n'est rien sans sentiment"*— Now notwithstanding they make such a pother about the *word,* they have no precise idea annex'd to it— And so much for that same subject called love.[4]

That was the adverb. For the adjective, there is an air of innocence and purity about Sterne's use of it that well becomes "the English Rabelais."

Bishop Warburton seems to have been the first to give him that name, as early as April, 1760, when *Tristram Shandy* was still new.[5] Warburton soon was sorry that he had had anything to do with the sinner, and another bishop, Richard Hurd, once expressed the common and pathetic regret that "he does not seem capable of following the advice which one gave him—*of laughing in such a manner, as that Virgins and Priests might laugh with him."* [6] Diderot and Voltaire too, though they were not bishops, had Rabelais in their heads. On Diderot *Tristram Shandy* made the impression of a universal satire—Diderot, whose sensibility could be alarming —and he said of it, "This book, so mad, so wise, and so gay, is the Rabelais of the English." [7] To Voltaire, Sterne was the second Rabelais of England [8] (the first being Swift), and *Tristram Shandy* was "continual buffoonery in the vein of Scarron." [9]

People take what they want. In France Sterne was seen as both a jester and a profound philosopher, and his sentiments were thought charming.[10] In Germany numerous Sterneian cults were founded, the *Sentimental Journey* became the holy testament of the sentimental rage, and in general Sterne was—by those who liked him—embraced with organised enthusiasm and an idiotic solemnity.[11] In England also, by the beginning of the nineteenth century, it was clear what people wanted out of Sterne. They wanted *Beauties*—that is to say, *Pretties*—and they wanted sentiment, plenty of it. Perhaps Dr. John Ferriar is as good a straw man as any to set up at the crossroads where the ghost of Sterne was guided out of the highway of comedy into the rutted lane of bathos. Ferriar had the goodness to commend Sterne's "antic wit," [12] but he seems to have tried to redeem his own consuming taste for *curiosa* by the complaint that "Sterne . . . contrives to degrade some of his most solemn passages by a vicious levity." [13]

It is apparently taken for granted by English critics down through Saintsbury himself that Sterne was not a gentleman, and that this conclusion is of at least a little literary importance. But the accusation that, whether tacit or expressed, drowns out all others, is that the reader has been cheated. We want to cry, and Sterne spoils the fun; we want to be properly moved by what we think rightly moving, and Sterne crashes into the middle of our mood with a smutty petard or else a ruinous lurch of uncontrolled emotion. Thackeray does not trust him, and feels uncomfortably that Sterne is always looking into his face to see the effect; but he is relieved on coming upon the Ass of Lyons in *Tristram Shandy*: at last he feels that he has found real sentiment.[14] H. D. Traill sympathetically expects to weep, but he is bewildered by what he thinks of as Sterne's blundering touch.[15] According to Leslie Stephen, "one grows angry when he spoils a graceful scene by some prurient double meaning." [16] And the other day, Mr. Cyril Connolly wrote of

> the terrible flaw which dominated Sterne's sensibility, the habit of luxuriating in emotion he thinks creditable, that turns his sympathy to self-congratulation and sets a smirk on all his tenderness.[17]

What nobody wants, what nobody can with any comfort believe in, it seems, is a thorough jester. Yet we can conceive of thorough egoists, and of actors to whom the world is a stage, for we are shadowed in our own most generous moments by the consciousness of virtue, and when the Furies are upon us we are not thoughtless of our posture. A thorough jester, however diabolical a phenomenon, is a human being; when you whip him he smarts. He differs from most of us in that he is so lightly constituted as to be able to make free with everything, and to find his chief pleasure in doing so.

The question was sentimentality; and a denial of the sentimentality that has been attached to Sterne would depend upon the material that had been used for the accusation. This is a matter of reading. On what terms does the writer entertain his reader? what does he say, and what is the effect of it? To see what he did with sentiment and, so far as possible, what sentiment did with him, it will be necessary to take a journey in the tracks of Sterne. The reader is invited along.

2

The First Inn: Tristram Shandy

1. Trappings—2. Tales

1

E VERYTHING in this world, *said my father*, is big with jest,—and has wit in it, and instruction too,—if we can but find it out." [1] This is not the only hint Sterne gives us of what we lose by a literal and incurious habit of mind. When, with the publication of the first two volumes of *Tristram Shandy*, at the beginning of 1760, he first walked in among his countrymen and made himself known and at home, it was as a whimsical wit and humorist. Nobody doubted. But all writing makes serious demands upon a reader— the chief one being that the reader read what is written; sooner or later the eyes glaze, a cue is missed, then another, until the dreaming brain begins to make its own book, and the writer had better have spent his time hoeing a garden. In the light of his later reputation it is discouraging to remember that Sterne did his best, without spoiling his joke, to remind the reader that his purpose was to amuse.

——Certainly, if there is any dependence upon Logic, and that I am not blinded by self-love, there must be something of true genius about me, merely upon this symptom of it, that I do not know what envy is: for never do I hit upon any invention or device which tendeth to the furtherance of good writing, but I instantly make it public; willing that all mankind should write as well as myself.
——Which they certainly will, when they think as little. [2]

What does the literal mind do when confronted by a passage

like this one? Does it notice that the last sentence is not an anti-climax? Does it take warning when warning is given with an almost flatfooted bluntness? Or does it simply decide to believe when it wants to believe?

In Sterne's use of the trimmings and commonplaces of the sentimental style, are all the keys we need to the character of the feelings advertised. There is no mystery, nor was there any intended.

Tristram Shandy introduces us to the histrionic powers of our man of feeling, to the hand over the heart, the bended knee, the hand clapped to the head, and the passionate outcry. The book is full of apostrophes and invocations—to Heaven, to Slawkenbergius, to the stars and the critics and Mrs. Wadman—and, like the *O's* and *Alas's*, they are all comic. Sterne is not disposed to enjoy them all to himself; he jogs the laggard reader. "Unhappy Mrs. Wadman!" he cries, "—For nothing can make this chapter go off with spirit but an apostrophe to thee—." [3] And again, when the French commissary tells him that though he is going by boat on the Rhone he must pay for the next post by land:

> *Bon Dieu!* what, pay for the way I go! and for the way I do *not* go!
> —C'est tout egal; replied the commissary—
> —The devil it is! said I—but I will go to ten thousand Bastiles first—
> *O England! England!* thou land of liberty, and climate of good sense, thou tenderest of mothers—and gentlest of nurses, cried I, kneeling upon one knee, as I was beginning my apostrophe.
> When the director of Madam LeBlanc's conscience coming in at that instant, and seeing a person in black, with a face as pale as ashes, at his devotions—looking still paler by the contrast and distress of his drapery—ask'd, if I stood in want of the aids of the church——
> I go by WATER—said I—and here's another will be for making me pay for going by OIL. [4]

And there is a wild moment when Heaven and later the chaste stars are called upon, and sensibility goes mad in frenzied farce:

Bless us!—what noble work we should make!—how should I tickle it off!—and what spirits should I find myself in, to be writing away for such readers!—and you—just heaven!—with what raptures would you sit and read—but oh!—'tis too much —I am sick—I faint away deliciously at the thoughts of it— 'tis more than nature can bear!—lay hold of me———I am giddy—I am stone blind—I'm dying—I am gone.——Help! Help! Help! [5]

It is not too much to ask of a reader that he remember this passage when he arrives at the *Journal to Eliza*. And it may pale the purple of the one rather teasing apostrophe in *Tristram Shandy*, that to the goodness of Uncle Toby.

Here—but why here—rather than in any other part of my story———I am not able to tell:———but here it is———my heart stops me t·· pay to thee, m·· dear uncle *Toby*, once for all, the tribute I owe thy goodness.——Here let me thrust my chair aside, and kneel down upon the ground, whilst I am pouring forth the warmest sentiment of love for thee, and veneration for the excellency of thy character, that ever virtue and nature kindled in a nephew's bosom. . . . . . .[6]

Since we are usually shown the author with pen in hand, we are now invited to watch him write on the floor beside his chair. No melodramatic gesture is quite useless, and any one emotion is as good a springboard to fun as any other.

In the references to his dear, dear Jenny he plays somewhat roughly with the fashionable sentiment of platonic love. There is nothing unnatural or extravagant, he says, in the supposition that his dear Jenny may be his friend.

Surely, Madam, a friendship between the two sexes may subsist, and be supported without——— Fy! Mr. *Shandy:*— Without anything, Madam, but that tender and delicious sentiment, which ever mixes in friendship, where there is a difference of sex. Let me intreat you to study the pure and sentimental parts of the best *French* Romances;—it will really, Madam, astonish you to see with what a variety of chaste ex-

pressions this delicious sentiment, which I have the honour
to speak of, is dress'd out.[7]

This amiably leering emphasis on tender and delicious sentiments
and on chastity and purity goes all through the works and letters
of Sterne. The tone of voice is struck once for all at the outset, and
he who has no ear for it is only to be pitied. As for Jenny, let us
not be such unmannerly detectives as to declare that she was in
actual life Miss Catherine Fourmantel.

———Do, my dear *Jenny*, tell the world for me, how I behaved under one disaster, the most oppressive of its kind, which
could befal me as a man, proud as he ought to be of his man-
hood—
   'Tis enough, saidst thou, coming close up to me, as I stood
with my garters in my hand, reflecting upon what had *not*
pass'd—— 'Tis enough, *Tristram*, and I am satisfied, saidst
thou, whispering these words in my ear, **** ** **** ***
******.__ **** ** **_____any other man would have sunk
down to the center———— [8]

Et cetera.
The "essence of all the love romances which ever have been wrote
since the beginning of the world" [9] is to be found later in Trim's
tale of a purely physical itch and an allaying hand; and the corporal's tearful "she was a good soul! as your honour will hear" [10]
does not refer to the more conventional aspect of the young
woman's philanthropy, for his honour has heard the tale of that
already. Sterne is capable of playing his tune in a cooler key, however, as when he gives us his lively little compendium of hyper-
romantic fiction in the story of two fond lovers—separated by
"cruel parents, and by still more cruel destiny—

Amandus————He
Amanda——She—"

going ignorant each of the other's course,

"He————east
She————west"

until at last, crying out

$$\left.\begin{array}{l}\text{"Is } \textit{Amandus} \\ \text{Is my } \textit{Amanda}\end{array}\right\} \text{ still alive?"}$$

they find each other, "fly into each other's arms, and both drop down dead for joy." [11] Such a story, he tells us, appeals particularly at that time in "every gentle mortal's life" when the brain is "tender and fibrillous, and more like pap than anything else." He protests his interest in the tomb of these two faithful, as a shrine to visit, but puts it aside (politely enough) in his hurry to go on to the Ass of Lyons and give it a macaroon.

Who can say, however, that the sentimental is not treated, in *Tristram Shandy* at least, with the respect that it deserves? It is even elevated to a branch of physics or metaphysics—I am not certain which. Slawkenbergius opens to the world an untranslatable view of "the involutions of the heart of woman," in a tale the moral of which must have a new word invented for it—"exquisitiveness."

> What can he mean by the lambent pupilability of slow, low, dry chat, five notes below the natural tone—which you know, Madam, is little more than a whisper? The moment I pronounced the words, I could perceive an attempt towards a vibration in the strings, about the region of the heart.——— The brain made no acknowledgement.———There's often no good understanding betwixt 'em—I felt as if I understood it. ———I had no ideas.———The movement could not be without cause.—I'm lost. I can make nothing of it—unless, may it please your worships, the voice, in that case being little more than a whisper, unavoidably forces the eyes to approach not only within six inches of each other—but to look into the pupils—is not that dangerous?—But it can't be avoided—for to look up to the ceiling, in that case the two chins unavoidably meet—and to look down into each other's lap, the foreheads come to immediate contact, which at once puts an end to the conference———I mean to the sentimental part of it. ———What is left, madam, is not worth stooping for. [12]

Sterne knows as much as any Slawkenbergius about the convolutions of the heart, and about the verbal threads and bodily contortions that are supposed to be the means of perambulating that warm labyrinth. It cannot be said, though, that he treats these mysteries with reverence. See with what diddle-diddle of the fiddle, what prut-trut-krish-krash-krush he leads up to the affecting powers of music, of the music of him who "fiddles to be felt,—who inspires me with his joys and hopes, and puts the most hidden springs of my heart into motion"; that's the time to borrow money of me, Sir, he says; that's the time to get your bill paid.[13] The Eye of Pity must submit to even worse indignities than the Hidden Springs of the Heart. When Walter Shandy—in despair over the winding of the clock, the use of his jackboots as imitation mortars, and now the crushing of his child's nose—flings himself across his bed in "the most lamentable attitude of a man borne down with sorrows, that ever the eye of pity dropp'd a tear for," [14] his arm hangs over the side, and his knuckles recline upon the handle of the chamberpot. The picture is a fine one, anyhow, and Sterne is probably right when he says (calling us "madam," as always when he is most mischievous), that a horizontal position is best for pain and—for aught he knows—pleasure too.

But the tears flow, do they not? Yes. If I have counted right, tears are shed in *Tristram Shandy* on ten occasions. Three separate tears are threatened but do not fall, and an unspecified number in the form of dew on a pair of spectacles are promised for the future. They are all pretty cheerful as tears go, and not one of them—no, not the most respectable—but has a dash of frivolity in its composition. Some of them—one hates to be brutal about it—are the merest farce; others are more sophisticated. There is Walter's tear over his son's prenatal misfortunes ("My mother, who was sitting by, look'd up,—but she knew no more than her backside what my father meant"); [15] there are tears in Toby's eyes for his brother's disordered brain, when his brother is only quoting history and really does not mean to say that he himself lived forty years before Christ was born; [16] there are floods of funny tears in the kitchen over the death of Bobby or the wonderful solemnities of Trim.[17] At another time Trim is interrupted momentarily while three carefully ticketed tears:

    1. "A tear of sentimental bashfulness"

2. "Another of gratitude to my uncle *Toby*"
3. "A tear of sorrow for his brother's misfortunes"
run "sweetly down his cheek together." [18] The finer feelings are gratified and Trim is soon continuing the sad story of his brother who, by marrying the Jew's widow who sold sausages, got himself not only a pound of sausages, but a sausage shop into the bargain. Uncle Toby, no less than Trim, has, as we are told in one instance, "a tear at everyone's service"; but for once we are cheated; "——he pulled out a cambrick handkerchief——gave a low sigh ——but held his peace." [19] We might have expected a trick, for we were addressed as "madam" only a moment before.

The fatal and coward thrust comes when Tristram makes his visit to the Tomb of the Lovers. His heart glows within him, with the perennial Sterneian glow.

> ——Tender and faithful spirits! cried I, addressing myself to *Amandus* and *Amanda*——long—long have I tarried to drop this tear upon your tomb——I come—— I come——
> When I came—there was no tomb to drop it upon.[20]

That was no gentleman.

2

Certain tales in *Tristram Shandy* are in one way or another concerned with the heartstrings. Whether Sterne even intended to pluck at those strings we may discover by looking.

We were speaking of tears. The subject most commonly relied upon to make them flow is death—though loss is what hurts, and to cry in condolence is to cry in remembrance of loss or in fear for present possession. Nevertheless Death gets the glory; it is so much more respectable a figure than Egoism.

How moving is death in *Tristram Shandy*?

Parson Yorick is the first to go, though only in a biographical digression, for he is alive at the end of the book. When he died, says the author, looking ahead, it was generally thought that he was quite broken-hearted.[21] Well, dying broken-hearted is still considered a generous thing to do; it gives the friends of the deceased something to say about him and a reason for them to shake their heads. The friends of Yorick—"though he kept up his spirits in appearance to the last"—saw their chance and made it good. "What inclined *Eugenius* to the same opinion was as follows"— and what follows is the death-bed scene, with Eugenius weeping and Yorick in full control of himself. Yorick, after thanking Eugenius for his friendship, admits that he is about to give his enemies the slip for ever. Eugenius tearfully assures the dying parson that all will yet be well and that there is still enough of him left to make a bishop. In reply, Yorick takes off his night-cap to show his head. The other sees nothing wrong with it, but is informed that it is so hopelessly battered by metaphorical blows that though "mitres . . . be suffered to rain down from heaven as thick as hail, not one of them would fit it." Yorick's last breath is a jest, and his eyes are lighted with a flicker of what was wont to set the table in a roar. "Eugenius was convinced from this, that the heart of his friend was broke." And lest Eugenius be somehow taken for Sterne, we are presented with a black page, a couple of Alas-poor-Yoricks, and a pointed reference, at the beginning of the next chapter, to "this rhapsodical work"—a phrase which the historian of words may grant or refuse the double meaning I see in it, without for a moment turning Sterne into Eugenius.*

So much for the art of dying and for the first lesson in the art of grieving. All the other lessons in the latter may be drawn from the tableaux which follow the death of Bobby and make as sprightly a vaudeville of lamentation as may be found in literature. And by the way, it is a pleasure to be able to remind the squeamish of the exquisite good taste with which our author keeps the corpse from home.

For three and a half blank lines, Uncle Toby hums over a letter that has been brought into the parlour.

* Says H. D. Traill (*Sterne*, p. 171) "we ask ourselves with some wonder what the unhappiness—or the death itself, for that matter—is 'all about.' [A cock and a bull, said *Yorick*.] The wrongs which were supposed to have broken Yorick's heart are most imperfectly specified (a comic proof, by the way, of Sterne's entire absorption in himself to the confusion of his own personal knowledge with that of the reader) and the first conditions of enlisting the reader's sympathies are left unfulfilled." Sometimes, when the house is silent, a comedian must feel like giving up and becoming an honest citizen.

——he's gone said my uncle *Toby*.—Where—Who? cried my father.—My nephew, said my uncle *Toby*.—What—without leave—without money—without governor? cried my father in amazement. No:—he is dead, my dear brother, quoth my uncle *Toby*.—Without being ill? cried my father again.— I dare say not, said my uncle *Toby*, in a low voice, and fetching a deep sigh from the bottom of his heart, he has been ill enough, poor lad! I'll answer for him——for he is dead.

When *Agrippina* was told of her son's death, *Tacitus* informs us, that, not being able to moderate the violence of her passions, she abruptly broke off her work.—My father stuck his compasses into *Nevers*, but so much the faster.—What contrarieties! his, indeed, was matter of calculation!—*Agrippina's* must have been quite a different affair; who else could pretend to reason from history?

How my father went on, in my opinion, deserves a chapter to itself.

Chapter III

—— ——And a chapter it shall have, and a devil of a one too—so look to yourselves.[22]

It is as long and lively and amusing a chapter as any in the book; death is only a new background—a kind of wash, and anything but sombre—for varied illustrations of the two characters and their hobbyhorses, of Walter's deliciously pedantic rationalism (which is by no means all there is to Walter), and Toby's brainless good nature (which is not all there is to Toby). Having duly rehearsed, with meditative relish—and frequent interruptions—the classical arguments on the vanity of life, Walter goes into his peroration.

There is no terrour, brother *Toby*, in its looks, but what it borrows from groans and convulsions—and the blowing of noses and the wiping away of tears with the bottoms of curtains, in a dying man's room.—Strip it of these, what is it? —'Tis better in battle than in bed, said my uncle *Toby*.— Take away its herses, its mutes, and its mourning,—its plumes, scutcheons, and other mechanic aids— What is it?—*Better in*

[18]

battle! continued my father, smiling, for he had absolutely forgot my brother *Bobby*—'tis terrible no way—for consider, brother *Toby*,—when we *are*—death is *not;*—and when death *is*—we are *not.* My uncle *Toby* laid down his pipe to consider the proposition.[23]

With a shocking disrespect for death—after a few digressions, in one of which he deliberately leaves his mother standing with her ear at the door—Tristram exchanges the bottoms of curtains for the bottoms of aprons, to show us what went on in the kitchen. For

a curious observer of nature, had he been worth the inventory of all *Job's* stock—though by the by, *your curious observers are seldom worth a groat*—would have given the half of it, to have heard Corporal *Trim* and my father, two orators so contrasted by nature and education, haranguing over the same bier.[24]

Though Trim had neither wit nor rhetorical skill, he went,

straight forwards as nature could lead him, to the heart. O Trim! would to heaven thou had'st a better historian!—would thy historian had a better pair of breeches!
————O ye critics! will nothing melt you? [25]

The comedy in the kitchen must be read.[26] There is no use picking out details—the "green sattin night-gown of my mother's" which, followed by all her colorful wardrobe, swings into Susannah's mind with the word *mourning* ("'No,—*she will never look up again,*' said *Susannah*"); the complacency of the fat, foolish scullion; the by-play, and the interruptions of the author himself, all in key and chasing each other in and out of the scene with an admirable timing. But the high moment of Trim's eloquence deserves quotation for Sterne's comments upon it, both oblique and direct.

He was alive last *Whitsontide!* said the coachman.—*Whitsontide!* alas! cried *Trim*, extending his right arm, and falling instantly into the same attitude in which he read the sermon,—what is *Whitsontide, Jonathan* (for that was the

[19]

coachman's name), or *Shrovetide*, or any tide or time past, to this? Are we not here now, continued the corporal (striking the end of his stick perpendicularly upon the floor, so as to give an idea of health and stability)—and are we not— (dropping his hat upon the ground) gone! in a moment!— 'Twas infinitely striking! *Susannah* burst into a flood of tears. —We are not stocks and stones. *Jonathan, Obadiah*, the cook-maid, all melted.—The foolish fat scullion herself, who was scouring a fish-kettle upon her knees, was rous'd with it.— The whole kitchen crowded about the corporal.

Now as I perceive plainly, that the preservation of our constitution in church and state,—and possibly the preservation of the whole world—or what is the same thing, the distribution and balance of its property and power, may in time to come depend greatly upon the right understanding of this stroke of the corporal's eloquence—I do demand your attention—your worships and reverences, for any ten pages together, take them where you will in any other part of the work, shall sleep for it at your ease.

There was nothing in the words, he says; it was the immediate appeal to the senses that did the work (and how much not only Trim's audience, but that of Sterne, owes to the author's eye, to the innumerable brief sketches of hands and feet in motion, of pots, sticks, pipes, all caught at the moment when they tell more than hundreds of words could describe). "If Trim had not trusted more to his hat than his head—he had made nothing at all of it." And Sterne orders Trim to drop the dramatic hat again, for the reader alone, in slow-motion. "The descent of the hat was as if a heavy lump of clay had been kneeded into the crown of it." It fell dead like a corpse.

Now— Ten thousand, and ten thousand times ten thousand (for matter and motion are infinite) are the ways by which a hat may be dropped upon the ground, without any effect.——Had he flung it, or thrown it, or cast it, or skimmed it, or squirted it, or let it slip or fall in any possible direction under heaven,—or in the best direction that could be given to it,—had he dropped it like a goose—like a puppy—like an ass—or in doing it, or even after he had done, had he looked like a fool—like a ninny—like a nincompoop—it had fail'd, and the effect upon the heart had been lost.

Ye who govern this mighty world and its mighty concerns with the *engines* of eloquence,—who heat it, and cool it, and melt it, and mollify it,——and then harden it again to *your purpose*—

Ye who wind and turn the passions with this great windlass, and, having done it, lead the owners of them, whither ye think meet—

Ye, lastly, who drive——and why not, Ye also who are driven, like turkeys to market with a stick and a red clout —meditate—meditate, I beseech you, upon *Trim's* hat.

Needless to say, this is followed by a new chapter and one of those seamless and inspired transitions which knit the rags of *Tristram Shandy* into a flying carpet.

Sometimes one is tempted to agree with Diderot that this book gives the impression of a universal satire. But Sterne is only enjoying himself. To ascend to an "effect upon the heart" by means of a ladder of *ersatz* Rabelais is a small adventure that would appeal to any humorist, and no true humorist scorns to play with the serious business of his time. And Sterne's dramatic gift—that with a wave of his hand can bring the most commonplace fragment of a picture into whole and uncommon life—is kicked up by his wit to the pitch of farce. He delights in extravagant gestures and all sorts of melodramatic absurdities. He delights in a bouncing bathos. Could it be that his critics have misread the word?

We are still in the hilarious kitchen when Trim promises us the story of Le Fever. "Do tell us the story of the poor lieutenant," says Susannah, and all of us settle down for a quiet cry. The corporal begins, or so Sterne tells us, but immediately we are in a new chapter, the episode of Bobby is finished, the corporal is forgotten, and we must put our handkerchiefs back into our pockets. "I am a *Turk*," says the author apologetically, "if I had not as much forgot my mother, as if Nature had plaistered me up, and set

me down naked upon the banks of the river *Nile*, without one." [27]
Many chapters later, in the next book or volume, it occurs to Uncle
Toby that Le Fever's son would make just the governor required
for little Tristram. "A tear of joy of the first water" sparkles in
Toby's eye at the thought, and its brother sparkles in the corpo-
ral's.

> ——You will see why when you read Le Fever's story:——
> fool that I was! nor can I recollect (nor perhaps you) without
> turning back to the place, what it was that hindered me from
> letting the corporal tell it in his own words;—but the occa-
> sion is lost,—I must tell it now in my own. [28]

Writers can be remarkably careless.

For a man with such skill in the drawing of character and of
intimate, circumscribed action, the temptation must have been
strong to do a piece of undoubted pathos, and so not only prove
his mastery of the craft but win for himself the applause of the
majority everywhere—the multitude of readers and critics who
found sublimity in the pathetic, and genius in the man who evoked
the pathetic sublime. But see what Sterne did, in the story of Le
Fever, with the approved and favorite subject matter of his day.
It is as if he had said, "Look, how easy it is to do this sort of thing"
—and all along his sense of humor kept it true to his nature, and
his artist's sense of fitness kept it true to the book. Even more
likely, it is as if he had said, "You asked for it, Madam—so look
to yourself."

The story takes its time, and we soon realise that it is there for
the sake of Toby and Trim—almost incidental to the leisurely
depiction of our two whimsical sentimentalists, master and servant, with their military hobby, and their cosy surroundings filled
with tobacco and sack and toast. The author is, to be sure, as artless as usual—he asserts in the first paragraph that his pen governs
him, not he his pen; artlessness, we know, is virtue, in matters of
the heart. But only the stupid reader, for whom Sterne is certainly
not writing, can fail to admire the art that is in every line—an art
that is directed by an inward smile.

How important, really, is poor Lieutenant Le Fever?

Trim!——said my uncle *Toby,* after he lighted his pipe, and smoak'd about a dozen whiffs.——*Trim* came in front of his master, and made his bow;—my uncle *Toby* smoak'd on, and said no more.——Corporal! said my uncle *Toby*—the corporal made his bow.——My uncle *Toby* proceeded no farther, but finished his pipe.

Let us hope that all the tender hearts in England are waiting as patiently as Trim.

Trim! said my uncle *Toby,* I have a project in my head, as it is a bad night, of wrapping myself up warm in my roquelaure, and paying a visit to this poor gentleman.——Your honour's roquelaure, replied the corporal, has not once been had on, since the night before your honour received your wound, when we mounted guard in the trenches before the gate of St. Nicolas. . . . . . .[29]

And so it goes, in a retired military way, until Trim, to save his master's groin from the weather, leaves to do the reconnoitring himself.

My uncle *Toby* filled his second pipe; and had it not been, that he now and then wandered from the point, with considering whether it was not full as well to have the curtain of the tenaille a straight line, as a crooked one,—he might be said to have thought of nothing else but poor *Le Fever* and his boy the whole time he smoaked it.[30]

The corporal comes back with a long and circumstantial report, but the pathos is completely in the hands of Sterne, and his hands are cool. At the climax, we may notice, he is able to remark that the ring Le Fever kisses *twice* is tied round his neck with a *black ribband;* the color of a ribbon, and the exact number of times a movement is made, are carefully passed on to us by Sterne the painter as well as Sterne the clown, and the detail does not appear superfluous. At any rate, Toby is much moved by the story, and his single comment is as good as anything in the book.

I wish, said my uncle *Toby,* with a deep sigh,—I wish, *Trim,* I was asleep.

[23]

Your honour, replied the corporal, is too much concerned;—shall I pour your honour out a glass of sack to your pipe?—Do, *Trim,* said my uncle *Toby.*[31]

Toby's feelings are so strongly engaged by the misfortunes of Le Fever that he even gives up his hobby, for the time being, in order to devote himself to the sick man and his son.

It was to my uncle Toby's eternal honour,——though I tell it only for the sake of those, who, when coop'd in betwixt a natural and a positive law, know not, for their souls, which way in the world to turn themselves——that notwithstanding my uncle *Toby* was warmly engaged at that time in carrying on the siege of *Dendermond,* parallel with the allies, who pressed theirs on so vigorously, that they scarce allowed him time to get his dinner—that nevertheless he gave up *Dendermond,* though he had already made a lodgment upon the counterscarp;—and bent his whole thoughts towards the private distresses at the inn; and except that he ordered the garden gate to be bolted up, by which he might be said to have turned the siege of *Dendermond* into a blockade,—he left *Dendermond* to itself—to be relieved or not by the *French* king, as the French king thought good; and only considered how he himself should relieve the poor lieutenant and his son.

——That kind BEING, who is a friend to the friendless, shall recompence thee for this.[32]

After so involved a piece of serious nonsense, a melodramatic arm raised to heaven had best be quickly dropped. It is. But somebody in heaven must have seen the motion and clucked his tongue a little. The comedy of whimsy goes on, however, kept just on the respectable side of farce.

——In a fortnight or three weeks, added my uncle *Toby,* smiling,—he might march [meaning walk, of course].—He will never march; an' please your honour, in this world, said the corporal:——He will march; said my uncle *Toby,* rising up, from the side of the bed, with one shoe off:——An' please your honour, said the corporal, he will never march

[24]

but to his grave:——He shall march, cried my uncle *Toby*, marching the foot which had a shoe on, though without advancing an inch,—he shall march to his regiment.——He cannot stand it, said the corporal;——He shall be supported, said my uncle *Toby;*——He'll drop at last, said the corporal, and what will become of his boy?——He shall not drop, said my uncle *Toby*, firmly.——A-well-o'-day,—do what we can for him, said *Trim*,, maintaining his point,—the poor soul will die:——He shall not die, by G——, cried my uncle *Toby*.
——The ACCUSING SPIRIT, which flew up to heaven's chancery with the oath, blush'd as he gave it in;—and the RECORDING ANGEL, as he wrote it down, dropp'd a tear upon the word, and blotted it out for ever.[33]

An amusing conceit in the baroque manner. Strange to say, there have been people who objected to that tear. But why? Tears were in the air; and if Sterne, who could hardly have felt any queasiness at an oath, chose to send a sentimental one up by the Accusing Spirit, it was at least better than to leave the Recording Angel (like Tristram in search of the tomb) with a tear in his eye and no word to drop it upon.

It is worth noting that what follows this delicate operation is a new chapter, consisting of only thirty-five words, in which Toby finishes up the rest of the day's business, goes to bed, and falls asleep. There is no lighter touch in English literature.

The critics don't agree. Look, they say, at the end of the story of Le Fever. It's murder!

The blood and spirits of *Le Fever*, which were waxing cold and slow within him, and were retreating to their last citadel, the heart—rallied back,—the film forsook his eyes for a moment,—he looked up wishfully in my uncle *Toby's* face,— then cast a look upon his boy,——and that *ligament*, fine as it was, was never broken.——[34]

Stop! Stop! they cry. That's where it should have ended—with those ten perfect, those ten inspired words!

But are they so perfect as they seem? Regardless even of whether

[25]

they make sense, can they, in so jestful a book, be said to belong? At least, in their high poetic seriousness they are isolated; there is no parallel to them in either of Sterne's novels. If a careful reader has come to no other conclusions about his author, he has possibly discovered for himself that Sterne is a conscious writer—so conscious of tones and undertones, in fact, as to have put him more than once to the blush. Having set down those words (they came almost of their own accord, as such things do) Sterne had more sense than to erase them. Who would? After all, he was describing a deathbed. For a moment, for the length of a sentence, he was almost hypnotised by the pleasures of virtuosity; but he heard the false note at once, and instinctively resolved it into the true.

> Nature instantly ebb'd again,—the film returned to its place, —the pulse fluttered——stopp'd——went on——throbb'd ——stopp'd again——moved——stopp'd——

That was more like it. There's the Shandean vein. One could continue for a whole page of stops and starts, but not this time. "Shall I go on?" he asks. And in one word, the Comic Spirit, leaping from his pen, says "——No." [35]

To a critic, apparently, death has its attractions; a pocket-handkerchief is carried to be used; and a writer who breaks the common mould of deathbed scenes is either a rascal or a clumsy craftsman. It is odd that Sterne's novels should be acceptable in the whimsicality of their outward form; that Sterne should even be admired for originality and a certain fine carelessness of literary conventions; and yet that he should be expected in separate scenes or passages to behave like other men. To E. A. Baker [36] the tale of Le Fever would be a gem of impressionist art if it were not for that "rhetorical touch at the end," which spoils it. Walter Raleigh, in *The English Novel*, laments "the famous death scene of Le Fevre, marred only at the end by the appearance of the stage manager before the curtain." "Let those admire this who can," says H. D. Traill.[37] "To me I confess it seems to spoil a touching and simple death-bed scene by a piece of theatrical trickery." What is spoiled is an invention of the critics. Our clown, for all his virtuosity, has had enough of the deathbed; he is bored; and the critics, rather than acknowledge that such irreverence can be literature, accuse him of failure in an established *genre*. Yet these tricks, the humorous transparency of the rhetoric, and our intimate acquaintance with the stage manager, are—these same critics at a less sacred moment would agree—the spring of our delight in Sterne. And besides, as Sterne might say, one is amusing oneself with writing a book; one gets a hint now and then, an anecdote it may be, from a friend, or from Burton or Beroalde, and by playing with it for a while one may most agreeably fill several pages. Le Fever has served his turn.

A new chapter is begun on the spot, with Sterne confessing that he is impatient to return to his own story. So much for death; to a jester, life is the thing.

Any sort of life will do—that of a fly, for instance. To explain a joke may be excusable when the reputation of the joker is at stake, but it is a painful business. Let it be said flatly, then, and with all possible resolution, that the episode of Uncle Toby and the Fly is not sentimentality but humor. Toby, we are told, was "patient of injuries," though "a man of courage"; and though a man of courage, he had no insensibility or obtuseness about him, "for he felt this insult of my father's as feelingly as a man could do"; but he was of "a peaceful, placid nature"—so kindly that he "had scarce a heart to retaliate upon a fly." *Retaliate* is the exact word here; "retaliate upon a fly"—that demands an illustration, which no writer imaginative enough to have used the phrase in the first place could refuse to provide.

> ——Go—says he, one day at dinner, to an over-grown one which had buzzed about his nose, and tormented him cruelly all dinner-time,—and which after infinite attempts, he had caught at last, as it flew by him;—I'll not hurt thee, says my uncle *Toby*, rising from his chair, and going across the room, with the fly in his hand,——I'll not hurt a hair of thy head:— Go, says he, lifting up the sash, and opening his hand as he spoke, to let it escape;—go, poor devil, get thee gone, why should I hurt thee?——This world surely is wide enough to hold both thee and me.

[27]

A perfect short story, by the way, and the choice and placing of every word deserves notice. For the humor: one does not ordinarily speak to a fly; this is an over-grown one, which has tormented him cruelly; it grows to human stature as Toby addresses it, with biblical dignity, using the second person singular, and promising not to hurt a hair of its head; we may imagine Toby singling out a hair of its head; "go, poor devil"—in fact, "get thee gone"; and we see it fly off as only a fly again—"this world surely is wide enough to hold both thee and me." An indisputable fact.

The moral follows, and an account of the vibrations of pleasurable sensation which this incident roused in the author, when, but ten years old—"at that age of pity"—he witnessed it. (Ten is not an age of pity.) "I often think that I owe one half of my philanthropy to that one accidental impression." Then, having finished the "lesson of universal good-will," he draws, for both wits and dullards, a hand with the index finger pointing to the words: "This is to serve for parents and governors instead of a whole volume upon the subject." *

Anyone who persists in thinking that we were indeed being taught a lesson, will perhaps be so kind as to pardon our author his levity.

Some time later, in Christian charity, he recommends "Messrs. the Monthly reviewers" to the protection of God, and asks them, if next month any of them should "gnash his teeth, and storm and rage" at him (as some did last May, when the weather was very hot)—not to be exasperated if he treats "the honest gentleman" as Uncle Toby did the fly.[38] Meanwhile the fly story was becoming popular among tender-hearted readers. Sterne regaled them again, by offering his poor negro girl, "with a bunch of white feathers slightly tied to the end of a long cane, flapping away flies—not

* *Tristram Shandy*, II, 12. "It is a pity," says Traill with invulnerable solemnity, ". . . that Sterne should, in illustration of Captain Shandy's kindness of heart, have plagiarized (as he is said to have done) the incident of the tormenting fly. . . . There is something too much of self-conscious virtue in the apostrophe. This we feel is not the real Uncle Toby of Sterne's objective mood; it is the Uncle Toby of the subjectifying sentimentalist, surveying his character through the false medium of his own hypertrophied sensibilities." *Op. cit.,* pp. 169, 170.

killing them." This dish he set down with Trim's cordial tears among the pornographic sausages, where he evidently thought it belonged.[39]

It is not likely that the Shandean habit of confronting the grave with the gay, and the soulful with the prurient, was either an accident of Sterne's sinful nature or the horrid result of an incapacity to make his pen behave like a little gentleman—long enough, that is, to finish such courtesies as the sentimental reader thought it had begun. We know by *Tristram Shandy* that Sterne was able to keep in mind what he had written; and so we must suppose that he was aware of constantly dousing the head of the so-called Elevated in the horse-pond of the so-called Low, and that if the Elevated emerged looking as if it had been in a horse-pond, that was the effect intended. Only the fatuous would ask *why?*—with the portrait in their heads of some strenuous Yorick mapping out a program for the belligerent disposal of his infinite jest. But if *why?* is not the question, at least *why not?* is the answer.

In the tale of the Ass of Lyons there is no lachrymose corporal whose voice grows hoarse with philanthropic emotion, and who, in order to resume his relation of agreeable obscenities, must clear his throat and "aid nature" by striking an attitude "with his left arm akimbo on one side, and with his right a little extended, supporting her on the other." [40] This Lyons episode is at the other extreme of good nature, simple, careless, and all on the surface. It has been approved as an expression of sentiment, but it deserves more praise as a caprice. In the first place, an ass is not only a disarming animal with a countenance that begs pity from the idle onlooker, but it makes even a humorless person think of man. And in the second place, Sterne—as good-natured as any of us—was not interested in parading his humane impulses, but was intent on drawing the ass's picture, and letting it invite whatever nimble extravaganza might choose to come. The difference between Sterne's approach to the animal and that of any of our own contemporaries is clear at a glance; if Sterne talks to an animal or professes to interpret for it, he does so with none of our animal-story sentimentalism, but with an adult humor that springs from an essential preoccupation with man.

[29]

I have ever something civil to say to him [an ass] on my part; and as one word begets another (if he has as little to do as I)—I generally fall into conversation with him; and surely never is my imagination so busy as in framing his responses from the etchings of his countenance—and where those carry me not deep enough————in flying from my own heart into his, and seeing what is natural for an ass to think—as well as a man, upon the occasion. In truth, it is the only creature of all the classes of beings below me, with whom I can do this: for parrots, jackdaws, &c.—I never exchange a word with them—nor with the apes, &c., for pretty near the same reason; they act by rote, as the others speak by it, and equally make me silent: nay my dog and my cat, though I value them both—(and for my dog he would speak if he could)—yet somehow or other, they neither of them possess the talents for conversation— I can make nothing of a discourse with them, beyond the *proposition*, the *reply*, and *rejoinder*, which terminated my father's and my mother's conversations, in his beds of justice—and those utter'd—there's an end of the dialogue—

————But with an ass, I can commune for ever.[41]

There is the same deftly inconsistent treatment of small or common things as if they were large or uncommon ones, and the same murmur of parody, which we hear in the orchestration of all his humor. While being communed with, the ass is eating, with obvious distaste, the stem of an artichoke, and Tristram declaims in tragic style on the bitter lot of Jack. "Thou hast not a friend perhaps in all this world, that will give thee a macaroon"; upon which, like magic, Tristram pulls a paper of macaroons from his pocket and gives him one. The last words of the conversation finish, to perfection, the portrait of the jackass. The halter breaks short in Tristram's hand. The beast looks up "pensive" in his face— " 'Don't thrash me with it—but if you will, you may'— If I do, said I, I'll be d————d." [42] At this, some one comes in and beats the ass, the pannier in rushing by tears Tristram's breeches "in the most disastrous direction you can imagine," and after an equivoque the curtain falls with elaborate delicacy.*

That interesting rent in his breeches has dwindled to a "piteous" one by the time he is rolling along toward Moulins and piteous Maria. He draws up an Invocation to the spirit of Cervantes, finds his uncle Toby's amours running in his head, and in no time at all, everything is prepared for the next encounter. He is in a perfect state of "bounty and good-will," and each bump in the road only stimulates the kindly harmony which, so he tells us, vibrates within him. Whatever he finds in his way touches "upon some secret spring either of sentiment or rapture." [43] We have bounced off these springs before, and Sterne does not disappoint us. From the start of this episode we are in the desired mood of rococo foolery. Who but Sterne would have conceived the postillion as sitting in a line between Tristram and Maria, so that he would have to lean obligingly over to one side in the midst of his lyrical description of the maid? The postillion continues "with so much discretion and natural eloquence" that Tristram is on the point of questioning him and finding that, in the approved way of romance, he has fallen from some higher condition—but Maria distracts him. One sad story is enough to manage at one time. Maria, in gentle insanity piping away her service to the Virgin,

> made a cadence so melancholy, so tender and querulous, that I sprung out of the chaise to help her, and found myself sitting betwixt her and her goat before I relapsed from my enthusiasm.
> MARIA look'd wistfully for some time at me, and then at her goat—and then at me—and then at her goat again, and so on, alternately †——— [Shall he go on? Yes.]———

* Traill (Sterne, p. 164.): "Well might Thackeray say of this passage that, 'the critic who refuses to see in it wit, humour, pathos, a kind nature speaking, and a real sentiment, must be hard indeed to move and to please.'" Do these two humanitarians agree with Sterne that it is worth beating an ass to make a hole in one's breeches? Perhaps, dazed with gratification of their sensibility, they wandered off before the end of the chapter.

† Note this sportive pattern of alternation throughout. We have already seen it in the Death of Le Fever; it recurs in A Sentimental Journey, in, for example, the episode of "The Gloves":

"The beautiful Grisset look'd sometimes at the gloves, then side-ways to the

[31]

——Well, *Maria,* said I softly—— What resemblance do you find? *

He makes his excuses for this "unseasonable pleasantry in the venerable presence of Misery"—

> I swore I would set up for Wisdom, and utter grave sentences the rest of my days—and never—never attempt again to commit mirth with man, woman, or child, the longest day I had to live.
> As for writing nonsense to them——I believe, there was a reserve—but that I leave to the world.
> Adieu, Maria!—adieu, poor hapless damsel!——some time, but not *now,*† I may hear thy sorrows from thy own lips—— but I was deceived; for that moment she took her pipe and told me such a tale of woe with it, that I rose up, and with broken and irregular steps walk'd softly to my chaise.
> ——What an excellent inn at *Moulins!* ⁴⁴

Never leave anything to the world, Yorick—least of all a book. They may talk about it, but they won't read it.

---

window, then at the gloves, and then at me. I was not disposed to break silence ——I follow'd her example: so I look'd at the gloves, then to the window, then at the gloves, and then at her, and so on alternately.
I found I lost considerably in every attack."
See also the meeting with the Marquisina di F——, and with Maria again, pp. 93 and 104 below.
* Tristram Shandy, IX, 24. Walter Sichel quotes this "triumph of Sterne's pathos" down through the word "alternately," and (tear-blinded?) ignores the rest. (*Sterne, a Study* [London, 1910], p. 181.)
† Is anyone besides myself reminded of the lethal tenderness of Miss Beatrice Lillie?

3

Along the Road: The Jest in General

1. The Writer—2. The Preacher—3. Tomfoolery

1

THE BUSINESS OF CRITICISM is to look at the work itself. There is no reason why any work should be signed. An epic, a ballad, a system of philosophy, a cathedral, a pot, a peace treaty, a bridge, a novel, is interesting for what it is; and though it is finally the reflection of human mind and temperament, and made, like all created things, in the image of the creator—to ask *Who did it?* is to take one's eyes off the work and either concentrate on rewards and punishments or relax into the impudent idleness of gossip. Biographical criticism is glorified gossip, not only popular but respected among us (like the other qualified, or wall-eyed, kinds) as a type of our dogged irrelevance. But a work stands or falls by itself; that self is, if you like, the revelation of a man, but without it he does not exist, for except in his work he is forever unknowable. Every man is invented, moment upon moment, by his friends and enemies and by himself; he is caught and registered for more than a moment by his work alone; and if he makes anything that lasts beyond his years, it is the thing that lasts, and he himself is salvaged from his infinite unimportance only by reflection. A man is known by his work; poetry gave birth to Homer. And when we find ourselves preserving things because of the names attached to them, it is time for us all to go back to climbing trees and jabbering our eternal truths to the owls and the elements.

The excuse for talking about Laurence Sterne is *Tristram Shandy* and the *Sentimental Journey.* They happen to be labelled with his name, but so do the *Sermons* and many letters, including the

[33]

Journal to Eliza, mere remnants which the power of labels and our curiosity about our neighbors have given a ghostly factitious after-life. Even the scholars have been suspected of not reading the *Sermons*; the letters, though lively enough, are not like those of Charles Lamb, a work in themselves to rival his formal ones. But whatever is extant—if only the hairs left in a comb—may be used against us; and the dryness of a passage in *Tristram Shandy* may be denied by the academic on the strength of a tear in one of Sterne's letters. Not to flatter, but to forestall such eccentricities of wayward mind, we may as well stop off along the way and look for sentimentality in the life of Sterne—a life that for us is bounded at each end by one of his books.*

In that curtained period when, though a clergyman, he was doing political journalism at York, he showed no promise of any preoccupation with sentiment; but already, in the few pieces that have been identified as his, he was referring to Rabelais and Cervantes.[1] Here is a flicker of prophecy. For the rest, Sterne is in his earliest letters easily identifiable as the man we have seen in *Tristram Shandy*. The monstrous epistles to Elizabeth Lumley will be dealt with later; there is room to say in this place, however, that in explaining to Archdeacon Sterne his quarrels with his rapacious mother, he shows a heart untroubled by any reverence for the filial relation; his feet are flat on the ground, and his voice is innocent of the falsetto of literary cretinism in which he wooed his future wife. Such fancies as found regular hostelry in his head were at home in the rowdy library of his friend John Hall-Stevenson and the unreverend delights of Crazy Castle. The few letters we have that were written before the publication of the first volumes of *Shandy* —letters to the Rev. John Blake, Dr. Francis Topham, Caesar Ward, et al.—are those of a man burdened with domestic and professional affairs. They are fluent, impatient, and lightly peppered with irony and nonsense, but full of business and the restraints of a life that had been early imposed upon him. In 1760 he slipped out from under and imposed himself upon life.

* If, in the *Letters* and the *Journal to Eliza*, the reader finds passages whose tenor I have not dealt with at least by implication, the reader is welcome.

Now for your desire of knowing the reason of my turning
author? Why truly I am tired of employing my brains for other
people's advantage.[2]

The natural inference is not only that he was through with
being employed in the political feuds of York, but that he was at
the same time throwing off the chains of church and home. The
publication of *Shandy* was the deliverance of Sterne. He became
Yorick—expanded until he filled his role, fulfilled himself—and
gambolled over the surface of life until he died.

From the first his view of his burgeoning self, and the new
work of that self, is clear. In a letter offering the first volume to
Robert Dodsley in May, 1759, he says,

The Plan, as you will percieve, is a most extensive one,—
taking in, not only, the Weak part of the Sciences, in wch the
true point of Ridicule lies—but every Thing else, which I
find Laugh–at–able in my way.[3]

In his way. What his way is, one can discover only by reading
him. And the reader may know quite as much about the risibilities
of Sterne as Sterne himself did; more, in fact, for the observer does
the ticketing, while the man who laughs is the sport of an impulse.
But let the man of science chart the geography of Sterne's humor;
we ourselves are content to participate in our author's pleasures,
noting only that they have a way of being unexpected and of
obliterating the boundaries of custom and diplomacy.

Criticism from the outside drew Sterne apart from his work
from time to time, and made him try to winnow out from it a
few principles of which he could have been no more than half-
conscious while he was writing—for art is performance, not princi-
ple; not postulate, but the manifestation of understanding. Nevertheless he tried to explain himself, to reduce a dance to figures on
a blackboard. It was also deemed necessary for him to excuse himself—this footloose parson who preferred motley to the solemn
black. All these problems he solved in a Shandean way—a fact that
is gratifying to the sympathetic reader of his books.

[35]

I have rec'd Your kind Letter of critical, and I will add of Paternal Advice too, which contrary to My Natural humour, set Me upon looking gravely & thinking gravely for half a day together. Sometimes I concluded You had Not spoke out, but had stronger grounds for Your hints & cautions, than what your good Nature knew well how to tell me—especially with regard to Prudence, as a divine;—and that You thought in your heart the vein of humour too free & gay for the solemn colour of My coat— A meditation upon Death had been a more suiting trimming to it (I own it)—but then it Could not have been set on by Me.

Mr. Fothergil, whom I regard in the Class I do you, as My best of Criticks & well wishers—preaches daily to Me Upon Your Text—"get Your Preferment first Lory! he says—& then Write & Welcome." But suppose preferment is long acoming (& for aught I know I may not be preferr'd till the Resurrection of the Just) and am all that time in labour—how must I bear my Pains. . . .

But to be serious if I can—I will use all reasonable caution. Only with this caution along with it, not to spoil my Book;—that is the air and originality of it, which must resemble the Author—& I fear 'tis a Number of these slighter touches which Mark this resemblance & Identify it from all Others of the Stamp—Which this understrapping Virtue of Prudence would Oblige Me to strike out.—A Very Able Critick & One of my Colour too—who has Read Over Tristram—Made Answer Upon My saying I Would consider the colour of My Coat, as I corrected it—That that very Idea in My head would render My Book not worth a groat—still I promise to be Cautious—but I deny I have gone as farr as Swift—He keeps a due distance from Rabelais—& I keep a due distance from him— Swift has said a hundred things I durst Not Say— Unless I was Dean of St. Patricks. . . .

Ovid is justly condemn'd in being Ingenij sui Amator—and it is a seasonable hint to Me, as I am Not sure I am clear of it—to Sport too Much with Your wit—or the Game that wit has pointed is surfeiting—like toying with a Mans Mistress—it may be a Very delightful Solacement to the Inamorato —tho little to the bystander.

Tho I plead guilty to a part of this Charge Yet twould greatly alleviate the Crime—If my Readers knew how Much I suppress'd of this desire— I have Burn'd More wit, then I have publish'd Upon that Very Acc^t—since I began to Avoid the Very fault I fear I may have Yet given Proofs of. I will reconsider Slops fall & my too Minute Account of it—but *in general I am perswaded that the happiness of the Cervantic humour arises from this very thing—of describing silly & trifling Events, with the Circumstantial Pomp of great Ones—* perhaps this is Overloaded—& I can soon ease it.[4]

The italics are mine. Sterne was so much taken with this letter to an unknown correspondent that he copied out a version of it in what is known as his *Letter Book*. Here is the other draft of that portion on the Cervantick Humour.

As for Slop's fall—'tis most circumstantialy related, & the affair most trifling—& perhaps you may be right in saying 'tis overloaded—but not dear S^r because of the slightness of the incident—that very thing should constitute the humour, which consists in treating the most insignificant Things with such *Ornamenta ambitiosa*, as would make one sick in another place.[5]

Three or four weeks later, in a letter to David Garrick (27 January 1760—the first completely Shandean letter we have; from now on, the style and its man are established in both life and letters) Sterne says that he sent his book to the press, "hot as it came from my Brain, without one Correction." [6] Here begins the legend of the artless artist; whoever wishes to believe it may do so, but it is meant to be enjoyed along with the parallel myth that his work, like all good things, comes hot, or straight, from the heart. Throughout the letters he refuses to be serious. Catch hold of his arm and he somersaults out of the way; he may sometimes—because he abstains from winking—appear to be in earnest, but in the next moment, or in conference with the next person, he rattles his bells in the rear of his victim.

He can sweep the arts of serious biography and portraiture from their pedestal, and set up caricature to sit there looking bored as if nothing had happened.

> [*De Mortuis Nil Nisi Bonum*:] I declare I have considered the wisdom, and foundation of it over and over again, as dispassionately and charitably as a good Christian can, and, after all, I can find nothing in it, or make more of it, than a nonsensical lullaby of some nurse, put into Latin by some pedant, to be chanted by some hypocrite to the end of the world, for the consolation of departing lechers. . . . Inspired authors have done otherwise—and reason and common sense tell me, that if the characters of past ages and men are to be drawn at all, they are to be drawn like themselves; that is, with their excellencies, and with their foibles. . . . The ruleing passion *et les egarements du coeur* are the very things which mark, and distinguish a man's character;—in which I would as soon leave out a man's head as his hobby-horse.[7]

His innocence is flawless. No wonder he has no patience with the suggestion that he castrate his book.

> Be assured, my lord, that willingly and knowingly I will give no offence to any mortal by anything which I think can look like the least violation either of decency or good manners; and yet, with all the caution of a heart void of offence or intention of giving it, I may find it very hard, in writing such a book as "Tristram Shandy," to mutilate everything in it down to the prudish humour of every particular. I will, however, do my best; though laugh, my lord, I will, and as loud as I can too. . . .

His correspondent is Bishop Warburton. As for the pamphlets and other fugitive efforts that are being written either against or supposedly by him—he deplores their indecency and sighs at their injustice.

> These strokes in the Dark, with the many Kicks, Cuffs & Bastinadoes I openly get on all sides of me, are begining to make me sick of this foolish humour of mine of sallying forth

into this wide & wicked world to redress wrongs, &c. of which I shall repent as sorely as ever Sancho Panca did of his in following his evil genius of a Don Quixote thro thick & thin— but as the poor fellow apologised for it,—so must I. *"it was my vile fortune & my Errantry & that's all that can be said on't."* [8]

The joke is always best when it is understood, and Sterne knew that Warburton was fairly astute; he may not have suspected, however, that the bishop would be angry.

In "My Witty Widow, Mrs. F." he had perfect confidence.

Now I wish to God, I was at your elbow— I have just finished one volume of Shandy, and I want to read it to some one who I know can taste and rellish humour . . . know then, that I think there is more laughable humour,—with equal degree of Cervantik Satyr—if not more than in the last— but we are bad Judges of the merit of our Children.[9]

And (speaking of volumes seven and eight) he presumes that Robert Foley will share his amusement.

You will read as odd a Tour thro' france, as ever was projected or executed by traveller or travell Writer, since the world began—'tis a laughing good temperd Satyr against Traveling (as puppies travel).[10]

On the whole, enough people felt with him for the jest to have been worth the trouble. At Cambridge, on 19 February 1760, a student named Thomas Twining signed, with a group of his friends, a "deposition" testifying that *Tristram Shandy* contained the "best & truest & most genuine original & new Humour, ridicule, satire, good sense, good nonsense" that had ever come forth, and that ever would come again from anyone but Sterne.[11] In the same year Sterne had the pleasure of copying into his *Letter Book* an appreciation that had been sent to Hall-Stevenson by a clergyman in Geneva.

What a comical Fellow the author must be! & I may add also what a Connoisseur in Mankind! Perhaps if the Book has

[39]

any fault at all, it is, that some of his touches are too refined to be perceived in their full force & extent by every Reader. . . . I'd ride fifty miles to smoke a pipe with him, for I could lay any wager that so much humour has not been hatch'd or concocted in his pericrainium without the genial fumes of celestial Tobacco. . . .[12]

The rampant life of a literary lion was all that he had hoped it would be. London and Paris were a festival of dinners and battles of wit in the salons of the celebrated. But people are never satisfied with a man as he is; even among those who could not fail to recognise the genius of Sterne there arose complaints. In effect, he was asked to preach—either in the pulpit like a good divine, or in his books like a good man of letters.

The opinions of the *Monthly Review* tell the whole story. In February, 1761, they are already saying,

> We know you hate gravity, but you must pardon us one dull reflection . . . we will not scruple to affirm, that where sensibility is wanting, every virtue is deficient.[13]

By January, 1762, when they review volumes five and six of *Shandy*, they are seriously charging Sterne with immorality; these volumes, however, are not found quite so obscene as the former ones, and the story of Le Fever is said to do "greater honour to the abilities and disposition of the Author, than any other part of his work."

> Since Mr. Sterne published his Sermons, we have been of opinion, that his excellence lay not so much in the humorous as in the pathetic; and in this opinion we have been confirmed by the above story of Le Fever. We appeal to the Heart of every reader whether our judgment is not right? [14]

In February, 1765, the same conclusion is restated, and Sterne is exhorted to "strike out a new plan."

> Give us none but amiable or worthy, or exemplary characters; or, if you will, to enliven the drama, throw in the *innocently humorous*. . . . Paint Nature in her loveliest dress—her native

simplicity. . . . In fine, Mr. Shandy, do, for surely you can, excite our passions to *laudable* purposes—awake our affections, engage our hearts—arouze, transport, refine, improve us. Let morality, let the cultivation of virtue be your aim—let wit, humour, elegance and pathos be the means; and the grateful applause of mankind will be your reward.[15]

Who could fail to be moved by such appeals to his genius and his vanity? Who but a man of courage and steadfast humor? Sensibility and moral improvement had stood in full view of Sterne from the beginning, and had made their claims; he had not neglected to pay them the compliments of a jester. Now they were surrounding him, jostling him, and throwing into his face the responsibilities of his position in the world. But Yorick saved himself and the Reverend Laurence Sterne as well. No one should be surprised at his grinning lip-service to the heart and the proprieties. Yorick wanted to be at peace with the world; he even wanted people to like him—but not at the expense of his life, not to the ruin of his jest. There should be no trouble in understanding why Sterne went out of his way to dabble in sensibility. Draw the attention of a humorist to any subject you look upon without humor, and you get what you deserve.

A consciousness of the utility of the Pathetic is first evident in Sterne's letters when he writes, in 1762, to Lady D—:

"Le Fever's story has beguiled your ladyship of your tears," and the thought of the accusing spirit flying up heaven's chancery with the oath, you are kind enough to say is sublime —my friend, Mr. Garrick, thinks so too, and I am most vain of his approbation—your ladyship's opinion adds not a little to my vanity.[16]

The delightful complacency of this is in accord with the adroitness of that sublime passage itself. The rhetorician suits his style to his audience, and in the same year he is writing to his most intimate friend, Hall-Stevenson, "I . . . am busy playing the fool with my uncle Toby, who I have got soused over head and ears in love" [17]—and to Robert Foley,

I . . . sport much with my uncle Toby in the volume I am now fabricating for the laughing part of the world—for the melancholy part of it, I have nothing but my prayers—so God help them.[18]

The same correspondent is favored with a philosophical comment on his first Sentimental Journey, the one on which we left him in *Tristram Shandy:*

> —we must bring three parts in four of the treat along with us— In short we must be happy within—and then few things without us make much difference— This is my Shandean philosophy.—You will read a comic account of my journey from Calais thro' Paris to the Garonne, in these volumes —my friends tell me they are done with spirit—it must speak for itself.[19]

Sterne was susceptible to praise of any sort. The performer likes to be applauded, and does not halt an audience in the midst of its approval in order to question its understanding. When Sterne was praised for the delicacy of his feelings, he recorded the fact with a not quite ingenuous satisfaction; nothing was more natural, however, than for his next impulse to be distinguished by what some call a callous, and others a comical, indelicacy.

He was seldom unkind. The simple good-hearted negro, Ignatius Sancho, wrote to him to say that he had conceived the greatest affection for Uncle Toby and the honest Corporal Trim, and to ask that Sterne give half an hour's attention to West Indian slavery.

> That subject handled in your striking manner would ease the yoke (perhaps) of many—but if only of one—Gracious God! what a feast to a benevolent heart!

In copying this letter—one long compliment—into his *Letter Book,* Sterne generously gave it such point and polish as he thought it lacked; the alterations amount almost to rewriting. For the sentence just quoted above, Sterne, preferring that even in transports the pen should remain in place between the fingers, felt that a deceptively unstriking style was wanted; and so he recorded it for posterity as follows.

> That subject handled in your own manner, would ease the Yoke of many, perhaps occasion a reformation throughout our Islands— But should only *one* be the better for it—gracious God! what a feast!

"Very sure I am, you are an epicurean in acts of charity" is translated, with an interesting combination of modesty and artistic realism, into "Very sure I am, that Yorick is an Epicurean in Charity." And because Sterne is rather an exact man after all, a word about the *Sermons*— "In your tenth discourse, is this very affecting passage"—is emended to "in your 10th Discourse—p. 78 Vol. 2ᵈ is this truely affecting passage." [20] His answer to Sancho's request could not be more sympathetic.

> There is a strange coincidence, Sancho, in the little events (as well as in the great ones) of this world: for I had been writing a tender tale of the sorrows of a friendless poor negro-girl, and my eyes had scarse done smarting with it, when your Letter of recommendation in behalf of so many of her brethren and sisters, came to me—but why *her brethren?* or your's, Sancho! any more than mine?

Could he ease the burdens of those West Indian brothers and sisters even one ounce, he "would set out this hour upon a pilgrimage to Mecca for their sakes." [21] In the *Letter Book* he is somewhat more sober, and the gaiety of this asseveration is modified to "I would go a Pilgrimage to Mecca for their Sakes" [22]— more nearly credible but less typical. He says that he will do what he can for Sancho, and try to weave the tender tale into his book. The best he could do was none too good, as we know from the sixth chapter of the ninth book; but Sterne had the very devil of a time getting his eyes to smart to everyone's satisfaction, and much preferred the philosophy of sausages to the cant of humanitarianism. The latter was not half so funny.

In February, 1767, he is writing to Isaac Panchaud, "Im going to publish a *Sentimental Journey* through *France & Italy* . . .

twil be an Original." [23] All the nobility are subscribing for it. Can Panchaud procure him "the honour of a few names of men of Science or Fashion" in France? To his daughter Lydia he says three days afterwards that he has "laid a plan for something new, quite out of the beaten track." [24] What kind of book has he conceived? For his sentimental correspondents he has one story; for the others, another.

> I shall live this year at least, I hope, be it but to give the world, before I quit it, as good impressions of me, as you have, Sancho. I would only covenant for just so much health and spirits, as are sufficient to carry my pen thro' the task I have set it this summer.[25]

This to Ignatius Sancho, whom he would not hurt for the world. His friend Mrs. William James never gets a loose word from him, but the ease with which he puts on his saintliness for her sake is astonishing.

> My Sentimental Journey will please Mrs. J., and my Lydia— I can answer for those two. It is a subject which works well, and suits the frame of mind I have been in for some time past— I told you my design in it was to teach us to love the world and our fellow creatures better than we do—so it runs most upon those gentler passions and affections, which aid so much to it.——Adieu, and may you and my worthy friend Mr. J continue examples of the doctrine I teach.[26]

Sterne was indeed a dying man, but the *Sentimental Journey* betrays no concern with the world's opinion, and any doctrine that may be in it is a gay one.

> My *Sentimental Journey* goes on well—and some Geniuses in the North declare it an Original work, and likely to take in all Kinds of Readers—the proof of the pudding is in the eating.[27]

His publisher, Thomas Becket, who received this news, was honored with a view of the other side of his face; and if any of his readers were not likely to be taken in, in the second sense, these Demoniacs of Crazy Castle and their cousin Geniuses of the North were among the number. "I know not whether I shall write again while I stay at Coxwould," he tells the friend who is known to us as A. L—e, Esq. "I am in earnest at my sentimental work—and intend being in town soon after Christmas." [28] To another correspondent, the Earl of—, he pleasantly turns both sides of his face at once.

> I hope my book will please you, my Lord, and then my labour will not be totally in vain. If it is not thought a chaste book, mercy on them that read it, for they must have warm imaginations indeed! [29]

And to Sir George Macartney, on 3 December 1767:

> In three weeks I shall kiss your hand—and sooner, if I can finish my Sentimental Journey.—The duce take all sentiments! I wish there was not one in the world!—My wife is come to pay me a sentimental visit as far as from Avignon —and the *politesses* arising from such a proof of her urbanity, has robb'd me of a month's writing, or I had been in town now.—I am going to ly-in; being at Christmas at my full reckoning—and unless what I shall bring forth is *press'd* to death by these devils of printers, I shall have the honour of presenting to you a *couple of as clean brats* as ever chaste brain conceiv'd—they are frolicksome too, *mais cela n'empeche pas*—[30]

The writer is the man, and both are a jackanapes, and that is as it should be. Odd what a difference there is between Sterne and—say—Samuel Richardson, with whom he has evidently been thought to have something in common. But Sterne too could let a woman in on his fun. It is to Hannah that he says,

> I have something else for you, which I am fabricating at a great rate, & that is my Journey, which shall make you cry as much as ever it made me laugh—or I'll give up the Business of sentimental writing—& write to the Body.[31]

[45]

To the soul Sterne had written as long as he could. Sermons
were not in his line, and his only hack-work was done as part of
a clergyman's duties. Though he performed these duties (before
ill-health and authorship freed him) more faithfully than the
eighteenth-century divine of caricature, we can see him straining
to get away, and—by contrasting the *Sermons* with his other writings—can feel his uneasiness and boredom. Like most preachers
he found it convenient to borrow from the works of his predecessors,
and the borrowings were newly dressed out in weariness; it was
not the Reverend Laurence Sterne but Yorick only who, forgetful
of pulpits and at ease in his motley, could give the touch of his
pen to old rags and inner riches that was to make them dance together for two hundred years without stopping.

The limbs of Yorick strove continually with the cassock that
covered them. That his neighbors "generally considered him as
crazy, or crackbrained" was recorded by John Croft in the *White-
foord Papers* [32] and has often been repeated. Various anecdotes
are told to support this opinion—among them that once on a Sunday as Sterne was crossing the fields to preach at Stillington, his
pointer dog sprung a covey of partridges, upon which he went
home for his gun and left his flock shepherdless in the church.[33]
Whether that was madness or good sense is matter of opinion; it
is obvious enough, however, that his temperament was always on
the verge of unfrocking him.

The first advertisement of the *Sermons* appears in *Tristram
Shandy*, after Trim, with much posturing and countless interruptions, has finished reading aloud the sermon on Conscience. In
case the world should like it, says the author, the Shandy family
have in their possession as many sermons by the same Parson
Yorick "as will make a handsome volume, at the world's service,—
and much good may they do it." [34] When "The Abuses of Conscience Considered" comes out again (in 1766, in the fourth volume of published sermons) Sterne apologises for its reappearance
after its having been printed "in the body of a moral work, more

read than understood," [35] but says that here "it stands a chance of being read by many grave people with a much safer conscience." [36] Sermons (like private letters once the man is dead) he thinks of as a source of extra income. As for preaching itself,

> preaching (as you must know) is a theologic flap upon the heart, as the dunning for a promise is a political flap upon the memory:—both the one and the other is useless where men have *wit enough* to be honest.[37]

The way to the soul—in his days a more than usually mirage-like and mistbound territory—was through the heart, a fairly substantial organ, to which all the psychological mysteries could be provisionally referred. It is only to be expected that where there is a dislike for metaphysics, and a taste for what are called good sense and good feeling, religious writing should lean heavily on the third sister in the trio of Faith, Hope, and Charity. And it is rather surprising to find that the concepts of Charity and Compassion are responsible for only a fourth part of the sermons of Sterne, a man who is generally considered a specialist in such matters. He was able, without any signs of special frustration, to grind out many a sermon on such traditional and unexciting topics as Repentance, Faith, and Pride.

If anything is common to his pastoral treatment of all kinds of subject matter, it is a certain theatricality. Thomas Gray, who was one of the best critics we have had, wrote to his friend Wharton,

> have you read his Sermons (with his own comic figure at the head of them)? they are in the style I think most proper for the Pulpit, & shew a very strong imagination & a sensible heart: but you see him often tottering on the verge of laughter, & ready to throw his perriwig in the face of his audience.[38]

The humor is sometimes undeniable; I wish that like Gray I could see laughter often about to break over the congregation. But something I do see, and that is Yorick sweating in his robes and longing to run away to a place where he can move freely and talk like himself.

Religion is unbearable until it has been polished and bright-

[47]

ened up, though the clergyman is constrained to shade its light again. In "The House of Feasting and the House of Mourning Described," Sterne preaches on the text of *Ecclesiastes*, vii, 2, 3: "It is better to go to the house of mourning, than to go to the house of feasting," etc. "That," he begins, "I deny"—

> Are the sad accidents of life, and the uncheery hours which perpetually overtake us, are they not enough, but we must sally forth in quest of them,—belie our own hearts, and say as our text would have us, that they are better than those of joy? did the Best of Beings send us into the world for this end—to go weeping through it,—to vex and shorten a life short and vexatious enough already? [39]

But before long his calling has interposed itself, and he concludes that the house of mourning is "fruitful in virtue, and becomes the occasion of . . . much good"; the

> light and easy heart, which never knew what it was to think before, how pensive it is now, how soft, how susceptible, how full of religious impressions, how deeply it is smitten with sense and with a love of virtue.[40]

A man who was in earnest here would have difficulty in writing a Death of Bobby; the Yorick who made a joke of mourning would find this rubbish as easy to scribble off as his own name.

His bowels of compassion, though, would betray a certain constriction. They do. In "Philanthropy Recommended" he takes the part of the Good Samaritan and imagines his soliloquy over the prostrate victim.

> Had I known him, possibly I should have had cause to love and pity him the more—for aught I know, he is some one of uncommon merit, whose life is rendered still more precious, as the lives and happiness of others may be involved in it: perhaps at this instant that he lies here forsaken, in all this misery, a whole virtuous family is joyfully looking for his return. . . .[41]

This measured compassion is familiar enough, but it is worlds away from humanity as we, and those we call sentimental, com-

[48]

monly define it. When the heart goes out by such genteel calculation to persons of merit and virtue, we need not fear that it will
lose itself and never return. Actually Sterne's heart remained in
its place, patiently ticking off the drab and dutiful minutes. "Some
such thoughts as these," he concludes, must have been the Samaritan's:

> Let me then hasten to supply those tender offices of binding
> up his wounds, and carrying him to a place of safety—or if
> that assistance comes too late, I shall comfort him at least
> in his last hour—and, if I can do nothing else,—I shall soften
> his misfortunes by dropping a tear of pity over them.[42]

There is nothing to prevent a jester from playing the man of
sensibility without a smile. The only trouble is that since the
actor must think up the words, and since the words and the part
are in every way foreign to his nature, the play falls flat. We have
seen Sterne make undoubted fun of the hackneyed tear of pity;
we know that he is able consistently to make his characters talk
like human beings. That he fails here is owing to the stubborn
nature of language, which responds, like the material of any other
art, only to the comprehending and sympathetic hand. Language
declined to rise to the occasion, for nothing was summoned forth
in the first place but an echo. And yet to call this passing whim a
failure is beside the point; there is no question of success or failure
when, by an impulse, a man slips a mask on his face, parades in
it for a while, and then throws it into the air. Sterne performed in
this same mask for Elizabeth Lumley and Eliza Draper, until he
grew tired of the thing. Why not? A jester is not required to be serious; and the best of writers, in the course of a lifetime, finds occasion for not expressing himself. If you are looking for literature,
for Sterne competently expressed, go to his novels. The *Sermons*
are second-rate because Sterne is Yorick, and Yorick, tied to the
pulpit, is not half trying.

There are a few lines in "The Levite and his Concubine" in
which charity for once comes to life as the child of tolerance and
delight in living. The real man breaks through with impatience,
and the language is that of Yorick. He has been quoting the

text, how the Levite goes after his unfaithful concubine "to speak friendly to her," and how she comes up to him and brings him to her father's house: "and when the father of the damsel saw him, he rejoiced to meet him." [43]

> A most sentimental group! you'll say: and so it is, my good commentator, the world talks of everything: give but the outlines of a story,————let *Spleen* or *Prudery* snatch the pencil, and they will finish it with so many hard strokes, and with so dirty a colouring, that *Candour* and *Courtesy* will sit in torture as they look at it.[44]

Even its patron admits that the word *sentimental* is subject to irony and ridicule. What Sterne is defending is not a word but the impulse of friendliness and courtesy, and the candor that will live and let live, and refuse to be fenced in by custom and ill-humor. Yorick knew the names and faces of the enemy that lurked along his wilfully twisting road.

While he preached he had to stay in one place, and to assert himself could do no more than give a kick or two within the folds of his surplice. He could loosen the grip of his vocation by re-defining it. *Joy*, he says in one sermon, is (when it is good and kindly) "another name for religion." [45] *Wisdom* is still another.[46] The vaguer the idea, the less oppressive the thing. Yet only the dull aspire to be wise; what Yorick wants is to be merry. Thus speaks a lukewarm father and an impious son:

> Gentle spirits, light up the pavilion with a sacred fire; and parental love and filial piety, lead in the mask with riot and wild festivity!— Was it not for this that GOD gave man music to strike upon the kindly passions; that Nature taught the feet to dance to its movements, and, as chief governess of the feast, poured forth wine into the goblet, to crown it with gladness? [47]

By taking care, one may cut a caper in the pulpit that will look almost like a casual shifting of the feet. Yorick luxuriously imag-ines "the sad Items" of the Prodigal's extravagance and folly— among them "that a whore of Babylon had swallowed his best

pearl, and anointed the whole city with his balm of Gilead." [48]
He advises us to send our son abroad, but with a man who knows
the world and has "thrice made the *tour of Europe, with success.*
——That is, without breaking his own, or his pupil's neck." [49]
Such are the little frisks allowed a preacher. Once Yorick was
loose in the world, and scraping together his sermons for as many
saleable volumes as possible, he was hard put to it to prove by resemblance that he had fathered them.

> I intend to puzzle it [the world]—by some feeble Efforts
> in the work I am about—tho' was I to tell you the subject of
> the first sermon I've begun with—you would think it so truly
> Shandean, that no after-wit would bring me off—nothing ven-
> ture nothing have.[50]

3

Once *Tristram Shandy* had come out, the old duties were left
behind in the hands of those who had nothing better to do than
perform them. Yorick had a life to lead; call it a chase or a dance,
it was lilting and frivolous as the Shandean style in which the man
had found himself.

A jest is a verbal affair. What isn't? The Unknown, a mere word,
is as familiar as a second cousin; the Unseen was no sooner given
its name than the world was favored with a description of its face.
The philosopher dedicates his moonlit hours to sorting out life
from literature, and when the moon has waned, behold! life is a
book again. That we are all men of words the jester is vividly
aware; we could forgive him his knowledge, but we cannot forgive
him the delight he takes in it. If he only knew some limits! It's
most upsetting. But Yorick—upsetting? Why, Yorick is only a
rollicking fellow, skin-deep all over, and not at all prudish about
his hide. He is perfectly harmless, and no plaster falls, not a house
in the kingdom trembles, when he is amused. Not a heart breaks
at his juggling of words. He has only cracked some crockery in
one of the china-shops of literature.

Watch him play the man of his time, full of a decorative

decorum but yearning for virtuous and rustic simplicity. It is 1760, and he is writing, snug in his priestly benefice of Coxwold, to a lady named Macartney.

> An urn of cold water in the driest stage of the driest Desert in Arabia, pour'd out by an angel's hand to a thirsty Pilgrim,[51] could not have been more gratefully received than Miss Macartney's Letter—pray is that Simile too warm? or conceived too orientally? if it is; I could easily mend it, by saying with the dull phlegm of an unfeeling John Trot, (*suivant les ordinances*) *That Yrs of the 8th Inst* came safe to hand. . . . Lord defend me from all litterary commerce with those, who indite epistles as Attorneys do Bonds, by filling up blanks, and who in lieu of sending me what I sat expecting—a Letter —surprize me with an Essay cut & clip'd at all corners. to me inconsiderate Soul that I am, who never yet knew what it was to speak or write one premeditated word [see the first draft of this letter in Sterne's *Letter Book*], such an intercourse would be an abomination; & I would as soon go and commit fornication with the Moabites, as have a hand in any thing of this kind unless written in that careless irregularity of a good and easy heart. . . .
>
> I'm sure with regard to Discretion, tho' I have no great communications with her—I had always a regard for her at the bottome— She is a very honest woman; & I should be a brute to use her ill—only I insist upon it, she must not spoil good company.[52]

The beatitude of unpremeditation: no romantic poet knew better than Sterne what riches might be poured from the horn of this dogma.

A month or two later he shares the same mysteries with Mrs. Fenton, his Witty Widow. The style of "unfeeling John Trot" becomes "honest John-Trot-Style." As for the

> Stile of your female Epistolizers, cut and trim'd at all points.— God defend me from such, who never yet knew what it was to say or write one premeditated word in my whole life—for

this reason I send yours with pleasure, because wrote with the careless irregularity of an easy heart.[53]

Is it not amusing the second time? More so, even to the tenth. The ball gathers weight as it rolls downhill, covered with the snows of all his life; year after year Sterne glances to see if our eyes wink with his own, for he is not certain how many layers of it we know —and it is that tickle of uncertainty that prolongs the fun and is the heartbeat of the jest.

In 1761, Mrs. Vesey and his own *Letter Book* are the recipients of an exercise in the harmonics of feeling.

> That you are graceful, & elegant & most desirable &c &c. every common beholder, who only stares at You as a dutch Boore does at the Queen of Sheba in a puppit Show can readily find out; But that You are sensible, and gentle and tender —& from end to the other of you full of the sweetest tones & modulations, requires a Connoisseur of more taste & feeling —in honest truth You are a System of harmonic Vibrations— You are the sweetest and best tuned of all Instruments—— O Lord! I would give away my other Cassoc to touch you.[54]

Musical comedy slides by an arpeggio into farce. He writes to Garrick from Paris:

> Think not that because I have been a fortnight in this metropolis without writing to you, that therefore I have not had you and Mrs. G a hundred times in my head and heart —heart! yes, yes, say you—but I must not waste paper in *badinage* this post, whatever I do the next.[55]

From one actor to another, that is. The literary philanderer is capable of a kind of parody that remains polite and, while trifling, safely conveys a compliment.

> ——Well! once more adieu!—farewell! God be with you! in this long journey may no thorn grow near the path you tread; and when you lie down, may your pillow, gentle Sally, be soft as your own breast; and every dream be tinged with pleasures which hearts like yours are only destined to

[53]

inherit—so get well, dear Lady, merely not to lose y^r birth right *here*—& do not die to enter upon it too soon hereafter.

This is mere Selfishness; and yet I thought I was writing the most sentimental Letter that ever the hand of true gallantry traced out—and o' my conscience I still believe I am —but I wait to be accused before I justify. . . .

The gentle Sally T— is made up [the manuscript in the *Letter Book* shows that he had erased "dear gentle creature! thou art made of"] of too fine a texture for the rough wearing of the world—some gentle Brother, or some one who sticks closer than a Brother, should now take her by the hand, and lead her tenderly along her way—pick carefully out the smoothest tracks for her—scatter roses on them—& when the lax'd and weary fibre tells him she is weary—take her up in his arms.⁵⁶

This is a kind of parody, yes, but also a self-confessed exercise in the sentimental style, proving that the Reverend Laurence Sterne is as good a man of mode as any of them and can as gracefully proffer a bouquet of the flowers in season. The actor can always save himself—as he does here—by pointing at the paint on his face.

No one is forced to swallow whole—though anyone would be wise to taste—such remarks as Sterne makes to Garrick, on preaching, love, and sentiment. The word "enthusiasm" will take the reader back to that moment of transport in *Tristram Shandy* when Tristram vaulted into position between Maria and her goat.

O God! they have nothing here, which gives the nerves so smart a blow, as those great characters in the hands of G! but I forgot I am writing to the man himself— The devil take (as he will) these transports of enthusiasm! . . .

The French comedy, I seldom visit it—they act scarce any thing but tragedies—and the Clairon is great, and Mad^lle Dumesnil, in some places, still greater than her—yet I cannot bear preaching—I fancy I got a surfeit of it in my younger days. . . .⁵⁷

I have been these two days reading a tragedy, given me

by a lady of talents, to read and conjecture if it would do for you——— 'Tis from the plan of Diderot, and possibly half a translation of it— The Natural Son, or, the Triumph of Virtue, in five acts— It has too much sentiment in it, (at least for me) the speeches too long, and savour too much of *preaching*—this may be a second reason, it is not to my tastè— 'Tis all love, love, love, throughout, without much separation in the character; so I fear it would not do for your stage, and perhaps for the very reason which recommends it to a French one.[58]

The man sounds rational, and as always he talks about the materials of literature like a craftsman. Writing and living are different ends of an art, and to Yorick the virtues propounded by the writing of his time, and the feelings with which it is stuffed, are mere literary matters. Even a disaster can move him to no more than a literary gesture. In March of 1762, the Foire Saint-Germain burned to the ground and the merchants lost all they had.

Oh! ces moments de malheur sont terribles, said my barber to me, as he was shaving me this morning; and the good-natured fellow uttered it with so moving an accent, that I could have found it in my heart to have cried over the perishable and uncertain tenure of every good in this life.[59]

Why so could I, and so could any man; but the tears of a tragic sense of life do not come when Sterne calls them. This fragment of literary affectation is found in a letter to his wife; it is a sentence from a bright boy, proud of his pen and taking a ride on it, but remembering to set the scene and remark that the barber (like the boy) is a good-natured fellow. Decency abstains from joking over misfortune—unless it is fictional, like the madness of Maria; all in all, Yorick is best acquainted with the heart as a plaything, and he would rather play with it than pretend, without a grin, to a conventional decency.

I live altogether in French families—I laugh 'till I cry, and in the same tender moments *cry 'till I laugh.* I Shandy it more than ever, and verily do believe, that by mere Shandeism sublimated by a laughter-loving people, I fence as much against infirmities, as I do by the benefit of air and climate.[60]

"In the same tender moments" cheats the sentimental reader of his vision of mercurial tears. The art of Shandean living crumbles to glittering dust every image the world can form of Yorick as a normal human being. A consumptive parson is easy enough to believe in; perhaps his laughter is pretended—the divine courage of despair. But a moment later the picture dissolves and only the jest is real. The inconceivable is embodied, and the giddy spectator hangs on for dear life to his tombstone and his bed of pain. "Everything is rose-colored for this fortunate mortal,"—J. B. Tollot, of Geneva, is speaking of Sterne in a letter to Hall-Stevenson—"and whatever appears sad and sombre to other people takes on in his eyes a gay and smiling face; his only pursuit is that of pleasure." [61]

How far his pleasures led him is his own business. We have glimpses only of a jester, dressed as a butterfly with a sting in its tail.

Tristram Shandy, the "inamorato," asks to spend the evening with his dear Lady Warkworth:

> I am a fool—the weakest, the most ductile, the most tender fool, that ever woman tried the weakness of—and the most unsettled in my purposes and resolutions of recovering my right mind.—It is but an hour ago, that I kneeled down and swore I never would come near you—and after saying my Lord's Prayer for the sake of the close, of not being led into temptation—out I sallied like any Christian hero, ready to take the field against the world, the flesh, and the devil; not doubting but I should finally trample them all down under my feet—and now am I got so near you—within this vile stone's cast of your house—I feel myself drawn into a vortex, that has turned my brain upside downwards. . . .[62]

If all the world's a stage, it's a pity not to act as if it were. O ye good honest, earnest, fixed stone figures of people, will nothing prick you to join in the dance?

[56]

I have been for eight weeks smitten with the tenderest passion that ever tender wight underwent. I wish, dear cosin,
thou couldest concieve (perhaps thou can'st without my wish-
ing it) how deliciously I canter'd away with it the first month,
two up, two down, always upon my hânches along the streets
from my hôtel to hers, at first, once—then twice, then three
times a day, till at length I was within an ace of setting up
my hobby horse in her stable for good an all. I might as well
considering how the enemies of the Lord have blasphemed
thereupon; the last three weeks we were every hour upon the
doleful ditty of parting—and thou mayest concieve, dear cosin,
how it alter'd my gaite and air—for I went and came like any
louden'd carl, and did nothing but mix tears, and *Jouer des
sentiments* with her from sun-rising even to the setting of the
same; and now she is gone to the South of France, and to
finish the Comedie, I fell ill, and broke a vessel in my lungs
and half bled to death. Voila mon Histoire! [63]

His correspondent, Hall-Stevenson, was no stone image. David
Garrick, however celebrated on what we call the legitimate stage,
was perilously stiff in the joints; in talking about Sterne to Helfrich
Peter Sturz, Garrick summed him up as a "lewd companion who
was even more licentious in his conversation than in his writings,
and commonly drove all ladies away with his indecencies." [64]
Some of them seem to have come back for more.

4

Along the Road: The Jest in Particular

1. Husband and Father—2. The Great Lover

1

STERNE MADE A BIOGRAPHER'S WORK EASY for him by conserving his letters as literary remains. As early as December, 1761, he left a memorandum with his wife, "in case he should die abroad":

> Note. The large piles of Letters in the Garrets at York, to be sifted over, in search for some either of Wit, or Humour— or what is better than both—of Humanity & good nature— these will [after a selection of letters left in his bureau at Coxwold, and in a bundle in the trunk containing his sermons] make a couple of Vol⁵ more.—and as not one of 'em was ever wrote, like Popes or Voitures to be printed, they are more likely to be read.[1]

Most of his collected letters were written after this date, and with the same innocence of prevision. In 1767 he left another note for his wife, this one on the wrapper of his *Letter Book*.

> Fothergill, I know has some good ones—Garrick some— [here he scratched out, "Hall I fear not tho he has rec⁴ hundreds, they have been wrote most of 'em in too careless a way. besides he's carless."]—Berenger has one or two—Govʳ Littleton's Lady. (Miss Macartney) numbers—Countesse of Edgecomb—Mʳˢ Moore of Bath—Mʳˢ Fenton London—cum multis aliis— These all if collected with the large number of mine & friends in my possession would print & sell to good Accᵗ—

Hall has by him a great number wth those in this book & in my Bureau—& those above w^d make 4 Vo^{ls} the size of Shandy—they would sell well—& produce 800 p^{ds} at the least.[2]

It was his daughter Lydia who edited the first volumes of letters, and our view of his family life is barred now and then by her blue pencil. Fortunately she was not a subtle woman, but she is in our way nevertheless. She stands guard, smug in her borrowed fame, at the very door of Sterne's acquaintance with his wife. We naturally expect a love-letter; we are given four stupendous lucubrations, one of which (a good twenty-seven years after its supposed composition) palpitates almost word for word in the lovesick *Journal to Eliza*. Perhaps a chemist should be called in, but at present we are not certain whether these twice-told drops of the heart's blood were indeed copied into the *Journal* by Sterne, or whether Lydia forged them into the letter out of the *Journal*, which it is more than probable she had not seen. I suggest a compromise. If Sterne did not rework the Lumley material for his dear Eliza, then Lydia reworked the Eliza material for his dear Lumley, from an odd draft she found among Sterne's papers. Neither side will deny that Lydia was capable of almost anything but intelligent behavior, or that Sterne wrote from the heart by way of careful revision.

If this first letter to Elizabeth Lumley was actually written in 1739 or 1740 as we have it now, Sterne was the first person on record to use the word "sentimental." He was disingenuous about it from the start. The literary self-consciousness of the lover is too evident to argue about: a clergyman ought to get himself a wife; a wife must be wooed; and the current devices for the manufacture of love-letters are at hand, ready for exploitation.

One solitary plate, one knife, one fork, one glass!—I gave a thousand pensive, penetrating looks at the chair thou hadst so often graced, in those quiet, and sentimental repasts—then laid down my knife, and fork, and took out my handkerchief, and clapped it across my face, and wept like a child.—I do so this very moment, my L. for as I take up my pen my poor pulse quickens, my pale face glows, and tears are trickling down upon the paper, as I trace the word L—.[3]

[59]

As every writer knows, the ability to catch and record these emotional phenomena in the very act, and to place them in a selectively detailed setting, is proof of considerable artistic self-control. All that is wrong with this little *étude* is its unlikeness to life and its over-literary calculation. The knife, the fork, are laid down with too much care; the handkerchief is applied with too much verve and the word "clapped" is too Shandean; the looks at the chair are too many, and they have none but an alliterative need to be either pensive or penetrating; the author is impossibly doctor, spectator, weeper, and writer at once, and the tears necessarily trickle (is this the right word?) down upon the paper *before* he is able to trace the word L—. Furthermore, he rounds out his composition with the roses and jessamines with which he began—a rather obvious technical trick; and the final words, while sufficiently melodramatic, are sudden, fortuitous, and somehow unflattering: "Ah me!—But adieu—the vesper bell calls me from thee to my God!"

Since Miss Lumley herself did not call a halt to the performance, who are we to complain? The three succeeding letters, in a loud baritone, run up and down the gamut of sentimental platitude. As for the performer's affection, it must be inferred from the fact that he is leaving no phrase unturned in the language of romance.

> Yes! I will steal from the world, and not a babbling tongue shall tell where I am— Echo shall not so much as whisper my hiding place—suffer the imagination to paint it as a little sun-gilt cottage on the side of a romantic hill—dost thou think I will leave love and friendship behind me? No! they shall be my companions in solitude, for they will sit down, and rise up with me in the amiable form of my L.—we will be as merry, and as innocent as our first parents in Paradise, before the arch fiend entered that undescribable scene. . . . We will build, and we will plant, in our own way—simplicity shall not be tortured by art—we will learn of nature how to live—she shall be our alchymist, to mingle all the good of life into one salubrious draught. . . .[4]

Without society and its artifices, he would have withered and blown away; but he could pay court to the innocent goodness of nature.

Crouded towns, and busy societies, may delight the un-thinking and the gay—but solitude is the best nurse of wis-dom.—Methinks I see my contemplative girl now in the gar-den, watching the gradual approaches of spring. . . . Flora and Pomona already consider thee as their handmaid; and in a little time will load thee with their sweetest blessing.—The feathered race are all thy own, and with them, untaught har-mony will soon begin to cheer thy morning and evening walks. . . .[5]

Pity and forgiveness have their seat, by literary edict, in the heart of the beloved. The lover need not worry too much:

I have offended her whom I so tenderly love!—what could tempt me to it! but if a beggar was to knock at thy gate, wouldst thou not open the door and be melted with compas-sion.—I know thou wouldst, for Pity has erected a temple in thy bosom.—Sweetest, and best of all human passions! let thy web of tenderness cover the pensive form of affliction, and soften the darkest shades of misery!

Speaking of affliction, he is minded to say that he has "lost a very valuable friend by a sad accident, and what is worse, he has left a widow and five young children to lament this sudden stroke." The heart is a wild thing, and unmanageable in grief, and so: "For-give me this digression, and allow me to drop a tear over a departed friend; and what is more excellent, an honest man." [6]

If Miss Lumley saw the disquieting implications of all these cheerfully bogus gestures, they did not bother her. Sterne wanted a wife; Miss Lumley wanted a husband; the rest would take care of itself. By 1760, if not before, Sterne was writing to Hall-Stevenson, with commendable restraint, that he did not know what was the matter with him but he was more than ever sick and tired of his wife.[7] The letter was passed on to us by Lydia, who could not read its dog-latin and did not have sense enough to suspect it.

Because marriage and fatherhood are more or less permanent in their effects, one has to make certain concessions. At home Sterne was expected to be a good boy. He managed to live with his wife and daughter until he became famous as the author of *Tristram Shandy*; after that he was suffered to gallivant like a bachelor, except when the two ladies were in need of money or advice. Mrs. Sterne must have been a lively woman. After Sterne's death, Eliza Draper once said that she had news which corroborated

> what I had a thousand times heard from the Lips of Yorick, almost invariably repeated—the Widow, I was assured, was occasionally a Drinker, a Swearer . . . & Unchaste—tho' in point of Understanding, and finished address supposed to be inferior to no Woman in Europe.[8]

In his daughter, too, Sterne occasionally found the hint of something with which he might flatter himself. "My girl," he wrote to Mr. and Mrs. James in 1767, "has returned an elegant accomplish'd little slut." [9]

But let Lydia draw her own portrait. She had just been advised, a year after her father's death, not to set up for a wit, for such had been the ruination of the family:

> As to inheriting my father's wit I have not the least grain in my composition we both thought it an unhappy turn in my father—I look upon satire with detestation and I must own when we returned from france we were much hurt with the satirical things we heard in every company we went into, having lived six Years amongst people who know not what it is to be satirical—and instead of attacking any-body endeavor to make every one in the company happy and *never speak ill of the absent*. I am so far from being a *diseuse de bons mots* I think I never was guilty of one in my life.[10]

How could Sterne have stayed so long from a fireside that offered so much amusement? Perhaps he knew the lines by heart.

For his wife and daughter he had to play a part that gave him only a fleeting pleasure. We must go to the year 1767 in order to find what looks like a momentary desire to partake of their domesticities. They are living in France; he, ill in London, may be supposed to want company, to want to be taken care of. He simulates a call for help; but the call dwindles to an assurance that he is behaving like a good family man, and that his interest in women is platonic, or at most sentimental. He is not sure that he can persuade except by means of sentimental rhetoric. "Friendship," he tells the impressionable Lydia, "is the balm and cordial of life, and without it, 'tis a heavy load not worth sustaining." True enough, but to other than Lydian ears an unnecessarily sententious beginning. (With his friend Hall-Stevenson, for instance, he spoke an easier language.) "I am unhappy—thy mother and thyself at such a distance from me, and what can compensate for such a destitution?" This sounds more convincing, though our eyebrows rise at "destitution."

> For God's sake persuade her to come and fix in England, for life is too short to waste in separation [there speaks a man]— and whilst she lives in one country, and I in another, many people will suppose it proceeds from choice [there speaks a man who knows his wife]—besides I want thee near me, thou child and darling of my heart! [Now for the second act:]— I am in a melancholy mood, and my Lydia's eyes will smart with weeping when I tell her the cause that now affects me.— I am apprehensive the dear friend I mentioned in my last letter [Mrs. James or Mrs. Draper in fiction, nobody in fact] is going into a decline . . . she has a tender frame, and looks like a drooping lily, for the roses are fled from her cheeks—I can never see or talk to this incomparable woman without bursting into tears. . . .

He has forehandedly written her epitaph, which he copies out for Lydia, among whose accomplishments was a pensive droop.

> Say all that is kind of me to thy mother, and believe me my Lydia, that I love thee most truly— So adieu—I am what I ever was, and hope ever shall be [why not, indeed?], thy Affectionate Father, L.S. [Then he adds a postscript:] As to Mr.— by your description he is a fat fool. I beg you will not give up your time to such a being— Send me some *batons pour les dents*—there are none good here.[11]

[63]

The man recovers. Another epistle to Lydia in the same year is an artificial flower of the same tint.

> I envy you the sweet situation.—Petrarch's tomb I should like to pay a sentimental visit to—the Fountain of Vaucluse, by thy description, must be delightful. . . .
> Mrs. James is kind—and friendly—of a sentimental turn of mind—and so sweet a disposition, that she is too good for the world she lives in— Just God! if all were like her, what a life would this be!—Heaven, my Lydia, for some wise purpose has created different beings— I wish my dear child knew her— thou art worthy of her friendship, and she already loves thee; for I sometimes tell her what I feel for thee.—This is a long letter—write soon, and never let your letters be studied ones —write naturally, and then you will write well.[12]

If the adviser does not follow his own advice, he undoubtedly has his reasons. The casual reader of *Tristram Shandy* may be aghast to find the very phrases of farce and satire patched and hauled out for a serious letter; the reader who has digested his Sterne feels nothing but a curious pleasure—and he is not surprised that when Lydia and her mother shortly afterwards make up their minds to come home for a while, Sterne whispers to Eliza:

> This unexpected visit, is neither a visit of friendship or form— but tis a visit, such as I know you will never make me,—of pure Interest—to pillage What they can from me.[13]

At the end of the year he paints himself as the father again, in a letter to A. L—e.

> My heart bleeds, L—E, when I think of parting with my child. . . . You will laugh at my weakness—but I cannot help it—for she is a dear, disinterested girl.

Someone might have pointed out to Sterne that a fond father is at liberty to grieve over being separated from his daughter, and that no one will consider him an object of amusement for doing so, whether or not his child is possessed of any endearing moral virtues. Another piece of common knowledge is that a grown daughter may easily be persuaded to stay within a reasonable distance of her father, particularly when the daughter is unmarried and the father dangerously unwell. This our hero did not have to be told.

Both wife and daughter may be said to have gone back to France by their own desire but not against that of Sterne. "You never read such a chapter of evils from me," he had written to Hall-Stevenson a year before—

> I'm tormented to death and the devil, by my Stillington In-closure,—and am every hour threatened with a journey to Avignon, where Mrs. Sterne is very bad—and by a series of letters I've got from Lydia, I suppose she is going the way of us all.[14]

No such luck.

> She is coming, everyone says, to flea poor Yorick or slay him— & I am spirited up by every friend I have to sell my Life dear, & fight valiantly in defence both of my property & Life— Now my Maxim, Eliza, is quietly in three words—Spare my Life, & take all I have— If She is not content to decamp with that —One kingdome shall not hold us—for If she will not betake herself to France—I will.[15]

2

In the same letter to a nobleman in which Sterne implored mercy for the warm imaginations of those who should not think the *Sentimental Journey* a chaste book, he put himself down as a member in good standing of the Courts of Love.

> I might indeed solace myself with my wife, (who is come from France) but in fact I have long been a sentimental being— whatever your Lordship may think to the contrary.[16]

The sentiments, the tilting with fine phrases, were his specialty; mere body was brutal and a thing he said he abhorred—so as to give piquancy to his fleshly suggestions, and a cure of comic spice to the nonsense of the sensibilities. But is it necessary to say again that he was no dogged satirist? He was Yorick the jester, with no vocation but to trifle as it pleased him and to abandon, if he wished, a cooked-up love, and let it helplessly simmer in its juice.

> I am glad that you are in love—'twill cure you (at least) of the spleen, which has a bad effect on both man and woman— I myself must ever have some dulcinea in my head—it harmonises the soul—and in those cases I first endeavour to make the lady believe so, or rather I begin first to make myself believe that I am in love—but I carry on my affairs quite in the French way, sentimentally—*l'amour* (say they) *"n'est rien sans sentiment. . . ."* [17]

We need not believe that he took such constant care of the harmony of his soul, but he paid it considerable attention. Among his papers which Lydia says were burned after Sterne's death by her uncle Botham, were probably what John Croft calls, in his anecdotes, "a large Parcel of Letters of Love and Gallantry from Ladies of the first Rank and Quality." [18]

In his own letters, two cases of love or gallantry strike the eye with a large amount of evidence. The ladies are named Mrs. Eliza Draper and Miss Catherine Fourmantel. The latter may be disposed of in relatively few words.

So far as we are concerned, the flirtation with the singer Catherine Fourmantel begins in York when, on a Sunday in 1759, Sterne sends her "a few Bottles of Calcavillo, which I have order'd my Man, to leave at the Dore in my absence." [19] "My dear Kitty," the next note begins,

> If this Billet catches you in Bed, You are a lazy, sleepy little Slut—and I am a giddy foolish unthinking fellow for keeping You so late up—but this Sabbath is a day of rest—at the same time that it is a day of Sorrow—for I shall not see my dear Creature today—unless you meet me at Taylor's half an hour after twelve—but in this do as You like— I have orderd Matthew to turn thief & steal you a quart of Honey—
> What is Honey to the sweetness of thee, who art sweeter than all the flowers it comes from.—I love you to distraction

[66]

Kitty—& will love you on so to Eternity—so adieu & believe what, time only will prove me, that I am Yrs.[20]

Here is the philanderer pure and simple. He is followed by the lecherous preacher.

I beg you will accept of the inclosed Sermon, which I do not make you a present of, merely because it was wrote by myself,—but because there is a beautiful Character in it, of a tender & compassionate Mind in the Picture given of Elijah. read it my dear Kitty, & believe me, when I assure You, that I see something of the same kind & gentle disposition in your heart, which I have painted in the Prophet's—which has attach'd me so much to you & your Interests, that I shall live and dye your Affectionate & faithful Laurence Sterne.[21]

And the preacher is followed by the author, who persuades the dear girl to send off in her own handwriting a letter he has written to her acquaintance David Garrick, asking him to give *Tristram Shandy* a good word. However sweet it may be to toy with a pretty woman, fame is apparently sweeter. In March of the next year he is in London.

I have arrived here safe & sound, except for the Hole in my Heart, which you have made, like a dear enchanting Slut as you are. . . . I have the greatest honors paid me, & most civilities shewn me, that were ever known, from the Great; & am engaged allready to ten Noble men & men of fashion to dine. Mr Garrick pays me all & more honour than I could look for, I dined with him today—& he has promised Numbers of great People to carry me to dine wth 'em. . . . I thank you for the kind proof you gave me of your Love and of yr desire to make my heart easy, in ordering yrself to be denied to You know who—whilst I am so miserable to be separated from my dear dear Kitty, it would have stabb'd my Soul, to have thought such a fellow could have the Liberty of coming near you. . . . I am sitting solitary & alone in my bed Chamber (ten o'Clock at night, after the play)—& would give a Guinea for a Squeeze of yr hand—I send my Soul perpetually out to see what you

[67]

are a doing—wish I could convey my Body with it— Adieu dear & kind Girl, & believe me ever y^r kind friend & most Aff^{te} Admirer.—I go to the Oratorio this night. Adieu, adieu. PS my Service to y^r Mama.[22]

So it goes, with less and less time for playing at love and for calling out of his head the acceptable romantic diction. "I long most impatiently to see my dear Kitty. . . . I had a purse of Guineas given me Yesterday, by a Bishop." [23] There is nothing but engagements, dukes, earls; but "God will open a Dore, when we shall sometime be much more together, & enjoy Our Desires without fear or Interruption." [24] Whether the door was opened, and for how long, we do not know—nor even whether Kitty was much taken with her middle-aged admirer. At any rate, the courtier played one of his rougher tricks when he gave a certain dear, dear Kitty a scabrous immortality in his book.

The relationship with his chief Dulcinea, Mrs. Daniel Draper, was without question a hyper-literary one. Such evidence as remains from Eliza's own hand shows her to have been flattered, mildly fond, and finally embarrassed to the point of publishing what might be called an authoritative text of Sterne's letters to her, in order to head off scandal and forgery. Between a proud but casual early reference in a letter to her beloved cousin Thomas Sclater, and a restrained but priggish comment after Sterne's death, Eliza hardly mentions her epistolary lover. At the beginning she writes, "Did you receive a letter I wrote you from the Downs with a copy of one inclosed from Sterne to me with his sermons and Shandy?" [25]; and at the end: "I was almost an idolater of his worth, while I fancied him the mild, generous good Yorick we had so often thought him to be." [26]

We can imagine what a strain it must have been for Yorick to perform to the satisfaction of Eliza and this other correspondent, Mrs. James. It was a challenge; he accepted it. In the end he climbed down from the tight-rope and abandoned the *Journal to Eliza* because he was tired of the act.

The beginning is a hop, skip, and jump that we have seen before.

Eliza will receive my books with this—the Sermons came all hot from the heart—I wish that could give em any title, to be offer'd to Y^{rs}—the Others came from the head—I'm more indifferent ab^t their Reception—

I know not how it comes in—but I'm half in love with You. —I ought to be *wholy so*—for I never valued, (or saw more good Qualities to value,)—or thought more of one of Y^r Sex than of You.[27]

A month or so later (it is early in 1767), he writes what is meant to be a platonic love letter of sensibility all compact—though it is largely devoted to the splendid history of Lord Bathurst and his recognition of Sterne as a literary figure in the line of his old friends Addison, Pope, and Swift.

He heard me talk of thee, Eliza, with uncommon satisfaction; for there was only a third person, and of sensibility, with us.—And a most sentimental afternoon, 'till nine o'clock, have we passed! But thou, Eliza, wert the star that conducted and enliven'd the discourse.[28]

"Brightest of stars!" Tristram Shandy was meanwhile saying, ". . . —The duce take her and her influence too." [29] But Yorick was busy with a new plan. The peer of Swift ought to have a Stella. "Your picture," he writes from Skelton Castle, "has gone round the Table after supper—& y^r health after it, my invaluable friend." And again:

Dining and feasting all day at Mr. Turner's—his Lady a fine Woman herself, in love wth your picture—O my dear Lady, cried I, did you but know the Original—but what is she to you, Tristram—nothing: but that I am in Love with her—et ceetera——said She—no I have given over dashes—replied I——.[30]

That was a dangerous lapse into Shandeism. He makes up for it in the flood of second-hand romantic passion which so grievously puzzles the readers of his *Journal to Eliza*. Yet surely our jester must be allowed to come near dying for love; and how else is a jester

[69]

to manage such a thing but by shouting "Help! Help! Help!" and thrashing about in the current of literary fashion?

He is generous enough to invite Eliza to share in the applause.

> You cannot imagine how many admirers your epistolary productions have gained you, that never viewed your external merits. . . . The style is new; and would almost be a sufficient recommendation for their selling well.[31]

After she has left London for India he writes to her at Deal, and says of his letters,

> When you have got them all, put them, my dear, into some order.—The first eight or nine, are numbered: but I wrote the rest without that direction to thee; but thou wilt find them out, by the day or hour, which, I hope, I have generally prefixed to them. When they are got together, in chronological order, sew them together under a cover. I trust they will be a perpetual refuge to thee, from time to time; and that thou wilt (when weary of fools, and uninteresting discourse) retire, and converse an hour with them, and me. . . .
>
> I hope, too, you will perceive loose touches of an honest heart, in every one of them; which speak more than the most studied periods; and will give thee more ground of trust and reliance upon Yorick, than all that laboured eloquence could supply. . . .
>
> I will live for thee, and my Lydia. . . .[32]

The intercourse of souls is too narrow for comfort. The "loose touches of an honest heart," however, must never be abjured, whatever follows the declaration of them, for they are emblazoned on the motley he wears.

> Talking of widows—pray, Eliza, if ever you are such, do not think of giving yourself to some wealthy nabob—because I design to marry you myself.—My wife cannot live long—she has sold all the provinces in France already—and I know not the woman I should like so well for her substitute as yourself. —'Tis true, I am ninety-five in constitution, and you but

twenty-five—rather too great a disparity this!—but what I want in youth, I will make up in wit and good humour.

And now, out with it!

> Not Swift so loved his Stella, Scarron his Maintenon, or Waller his Sacharissa, as I will love, and sing thee, my wife elect! All those names, eminent as they were, shall give place to thine, Eliza.

"Adieu, my Simplicia!" he exclaims, with a sweep of the arm, and signs himself "Yours, Tristram." [33]

The affair was literary from the start, though its monument, the *Journal to Eliza*, is not literature because Sterne was not at home with himself in writing it. Of the letters to Eliza, the first is signed "L. Sterne"; the next two are from "Thy Bramin." The rest are from Yorick, Tristram, or the Bramin, with the exception of a few unsigned. The *Journal to Eliza* is, of course, from the Bramin, though one entry is signed "L. Sterne" as a means of identification. Eliza had agreed to send in return a journal of her own doings, and the stage was set for a private undertaking, part of which came to light decades later with the following preface, in Sterne's own hand, miraculously affixed:

> This Journal wrote under the fictitious names of Yorick and Draper, and sometimes of The Bramin and Bramine, but 'tis a Diary of the miserable feelings of a person separated from a Lady for whose Society he languish'd. The real Names are foreigne, and the account a copy from a French Manuscript, in Mr. S—'s hands, but wrote as it is, to cast a Veil over them. There is a counterpart, which is the Lady's account [of] what transactions dayly happened, and what Sentiments occupied her mind, during this Separation from her admirer. These are worth reading; the translator cannot say so much in favour of Yorick's, which seem to have little merit beyond their honesty and truth.

Though this candor is artfully tempered by corrections throughout the manuscript, the *Journal* is rubbish—not because the hysteria is false, but because it does not sound real. Sterne lacked the experience; and besides, he was busy with other things and grew weary of this one.

His illness, which kept him from society and from his serious writing, was a godsend to the *Journal*. Separation from Eliza is killing him, proclaims the *Journal*; though on the same day that he half bleeds to death in its pages, he writes with composure to the Jameses, thanking them for their enquiry after his health. According to his physician, he says, the attack was due to his having taken James's Powder and then gone out in the cold. Impossible, however, for a powder of that name would help, not harm him.[34]

On the other hand, the threatened visit of his wife was a real hazard. "O Eliza! That my weary head was now laid upon ["yr" scratched out] thy Lap." The head is not too weary that chooses a lap with circumspection; Sterne's was bothered, rather, as we note in the same entry in the *Journal*: "Employ'd in writing to my ["wife" deleted] Dear all day." [35] He seems actually to have thought of escaping to India in case the additional weight of his family proved too much for his quaking shoulders. There is an extremely rough draft of a letter to Mr. Draper himself in which Sterne extends his friendship to that gentleman, announces his fatherly love for Draper's wife, and asks if he might be of any service to her.[36] And in the *Journal* he says, with the accent of a fugitive honesty of feeling:

> My wife—[deleted: & I wish I could not add my Daughter (for she has debauch'd her Affections)] uses me most unmercifully—every Soul advises me to fly from her [substituted for "them"]—but where can I fly if I fly not to thee? [37]

Not only had he other concerns, but he was not in love with the *Journal* as a literary experiment; and the indifference with which he transferred passages from the *Journal* into letters to other persons—and the reverse—injures the sensibilities of most of his readers.

Having whipped his pen into a series of romantic spasms, more than one of them twitching in double-duty for Eliza and Elizabeth Lumley, he seems to have looked back over what he had written and decided that as a record it was far below Swift-Stella after all. There follows a stretch of news in which a council of physicians determine that what ails poor Parson Yorick is a venereal disease; his protests of long-continued continence are ignored, and he is pumped full of the vile medicines that the faculty prescribe. He explains to Eliza that only the "purest consciousness of Virtue" could have tempted him to tell her the story, and then settles down again to "hold a discourse" with her sweet picture.[38] Since a good anecdote should never be wasted, he copies this one almost word for word into a letter to Lord Shelburne, adding that he has "mentioned" the incident in his journal to Mrs. Draper.[39]

In June he is writing to A. L—e as if no *Journal to Eliza* had ever entered his head.

> I am as happy as a prince, at Coxwould—and I wish you could see in how princely a manner I live—'tis a land of plenty. I sit down alone to venison, fish and wild fowl, or a couple of fowls or ducks, with curds, and strawberries, and cream, and all the simple plenty which a rich valley under Hambleton Hills can produce—with a clean cloth on my table—and a bottle of wine on my right hand to drink your health. I have a hundred hens and chickens about my yard—and not a parishioner catches a hare, or a rabbet, or a trout, but he brings it as an offering to me.[40]

Not a tear drops upon the cloth, but a month later he works the pretty picture into the *Journal*, omitting to say that he is happy as a prince, and remembering to drink Eliza's health in place of L—e's. He does not continue, as in the letter, "I am in high spirits —care never enters this cottage"; the presence of Eliza, he swears, is needed to complete the paradise.

Within a day of envisioning a heaven-sent marriage with Eliza, he writes the draft of a declaration of amorous heat to the "Countess xxxxxx." The manuscript, which is in his *Letter Book*, shows the Bramine's name to have been afterwards substituted throughout. Hardly a trick in the sentimental trade goes unparodied in this letter. After Sterne's typical stylistic formula, the soulful right hand is made to seem almost (but not quite) unaware of what the earthy left one is doing, and when the performance is finished the left is victorious. The mischievous parallel to the language of the *Journal* itself is instructive. His mind is brimful of his Countess; and in his sad walks round the ruins of Byland Abbey, he has been talking of her with imaginary nuns and with his favorite apparition, the ghost of Cordelia. This hapless maiden spirit was touched, he says, at his account of his correspondent's gentle virtues, "and glowed insensibly, as sympathetic Spirits do." [41] Cordelia is willing to be hostess for any of Sterne's deathless loves—witness the *Journal*:

> I now want to have this week of nonsensical Festivity over— that I may get back, with thy picture wch I ever carry ab^t me —to my retreat and to Cordelia—when the days of our Afflictions are over, I oft amuse my fancy wth an Idea, that thou wilt come down to me by Stealth ["and catch me" he first writes, but then holds Eliza off for a moment of preparation] & hearing where I have walk'd out to—surprise me some sweet moon Shiney Night at Cordelia's grave, & catch me in thy Arms over it—O My Bramin! my Bramin! [42]

In the letter to Countess xxxxxx she is more than hospitable.

> This Sisterly kind Being with whose Idea I have inflamed your Love, Cordelia! has promised, that she will one night or other come in person, and in this sacred Asylum pay your Shade a sentimental Visit along with me—when?—when? said she, animated with desire—God knows, said I, pulling out my handkerchief & droping tears faster than I could wipe them off— God knows! said I, crying bitterly as I repeated the words— God knows! but I feel something like prophetic conviction within me, which says, that this gentlest of her Sex will some time take sanctuary from the cares and treachery of the world and come peacefully & live amongst You—and why not sleep amongst us too?—O heaven! said I, laying my hand upon my heart—and will not you, Yorick, mix your ashes with us too?— for ever my Cordelia! and some kind hearted Swain shall come and weed our graves, as I have weeded thine, and when he has done, shall sit down at our feet and tell us the Stories of his passions and his disappointments.

My dear Lady tell me honestly, if you do not wish from your soul to have been of this party—aye! but then as it was dark and lonely, I must have been taken by the hand & led home by you to your retired Cottage—and what then? But I stop here—& leave you to furnish the answer.—*a propos*— pray when you first made a conquest of T. Shandy did it ever enter your head what a visionary, romantic, kind of Being you had got hold of? When Lady xxxxxx sufferd so careless and laughing a Creature to enter her [the word "roof" is deleted and nothing substituted], did she dream of a man of Sentiments, and that, She was opening the door to such a one, to make him prisoner for Life—O Woman! to what purpose hast thou ex- ercised this power over me? or, to answer what end in nature, was I led by so mysterious a path to know you—to love You. . . .

A few more passionate exclamations (including an "Alas! alas! what a world do we live in") bring him towards the end.

Dear Lady, write anything and write it any how, so it but come from y^r heart, twil be better than the best Letter that ever came from Pope's head—— In short, write y^r Nonsense, if you have any—write y^r Chit Chat—your pleasures, your pains, y^r present humours and present feelings (would to God I had just now hold of y^r hand).[43]

Where are the tears of Yorick? Here in print, and as amusedly feigned as ever. The *Journal to Eliza* drags on in the intervals of sprightly living; and once Sterne is again rid of his wife and daugh- ter, the last reason for this rather long bit of acting—the possibility that it might be negotiable for a passage to India—is gone, and he salutes Eliza and, for all we know, forgets her.*

* The *Letters supposed to have been written by Yorick and Eliza* (London, 1779), 2 vols., which were acknowledged by William Combe in a list of his own writings, have been reprinted as Sterne's *Second Journal to Eliza*, ed. M.R.B. Shaw (London, 1929). They are not likely to fool anyone who has recently been reading Sterne himself. For an examination of their claims to authenticity, see L. P. Curtis, "Forged Letters of Laurence Sterne." PMLA, L (1935), 1076– 1106.

> Mrs. Sterne retires into france, whence she purposes not to stir, till her death—& never, has she vow'd, will give me another sorrowful or discontented hour—I have conquered her, as I w^d every one else, by humanity & Generosity—& she leaves me, more than half in Love wth me . . . —And now Eliza! Let me talk to thee— But What can I say, What can I write, But the Yearnings of heart wasted with looking and wishing for thy Return.[44]

His body was wasted, but his heart and brain—never. I mention the brain because those who are taken in by the *Journal* have been able to save their reputation for critical shrewdness only by picturing Sterne as out of his head when he wrote it. Some of these distinguished people had not seen the self-contained nonsense that Sterne was sending to his other friends during the same year, 1767; few of them, however, could be unaware that he was then occupied with his second novel. The *Sentimental Journey*, a work of exquisite craftsmanship, was being written and re-written at the same time as the *Journal to Eliza*. The manuscript of the latter also is full of corrections, though it pretends to be the frenetic utterance of a lover parted from the mistress of his soul. A dying consumptive who, during the same days and months that he kept up a painstakingly maudlin essay in balderdash, could write one of the most delicate literary performances in the language, was, however ill, more fully in control of himself than most of us are in our prime.

He was as nearly absorbed in the *Sentimental Journey* as he could be in anything. Not even from Eliza did he hide the delight he took in this work; but then he never prevented a jest from bursting out from the wings, cue or no cue.

> Were your husband in England, I would freely give him five hundred pounds (if money could purchase the acquisition) to let you only sit by me two hours in a day, while I wrote my Sentimental Journey. I am sure the work would sell so much the better for it [not "be so much the more refined"] that I should be re-imbursed the sum more than seven times told.[45]

To Lydia he writes in August that she and her mother ought to defer their trip to England; he expects to publish his "sentimental

[76]

work" before March, by which time he should be in town to receive them.

As to my pleasures they are few in compass.—My poor cat sits purring beside me—your lively French dog shall have his place on the other side of my fire—but if he is as devilish as when I last saw him, I must tutor him, for I will not have my cat abused—in short I will have nothing devilish about me—a combustion would spoil a sentimental thought.[46]

He is the Complete Author, completely the Shandean Yorick. Sentiment is amusing for what can be done with it. By December the affectation of unalterable fondness for Eliza and Lydia (both in the same way or in different ways—a Yorick has no time to keep these conventions straight) has reached its climax; after that it fails to amuse him. He writes in December to A. L—e:

I have great offers too in Ireland . . . but I have rejected every proposal, unless Mrs. S[terne], and my Lydia could accompany me thither—I live for the sake of my girl, and with her sweet light burthen in my arms, I could get up fast the hill of preferment, if I chose it—but without my Lydia, if a mitre was offered me, it would sit uneasy upon my brow.[47]

In the *Journal*, under the third of August, we read:

I cannot take any step unless I had thee my Eliza for whose sake I live, to consult with—& till the road is open for me as my heart wishes to advance—with thy sweet light Burden in my Arms, I could get up fast the hill of preferment, if I chose it—but without thee I feel Lifeless—and if a Mitre was offer'd me, I would not have it, till I could have thee too, to make it sit easy upon my brow.[48]

The feelings in general, to the horror of good people everywhere, remain the chief victims of his wit. The following nugget comes from a letter to Sir William Stanhope, who was not a specially good person.

The body guides you—the mind me.—I have wrote the most whimsical letter to a lady that was ever read, and talk'd of

[77]

body and soul too—I said she had made me vain, by saying she was mine more than ever woman was—but she is not the lady of Bond-street nor ———— square, nor the lady who supp'd with me in Bond-street on scollop'd oysters, and other such things—nor did she ever go *tete-a-tete* with me to Salt Hill.— Enough of such nonsense— The past is over—and I can justify myself unto myself—can you do as much?—No faith!—"You can feel!" Aye so can my cat, when he hears a female cater-wauling on the house top—but caterwauling disgusts me. I had rather raise a gentle flame, than have a different one raised in me.—Now, I take heav'n to witness, after all this *badinage* my heart is innocent—and the sporting of my pen is equal, just equal, to what I did in my boyish days, when I got astride of a stick, and gallop'd away— The truth is this—that my pen governs me—not me my pen.[49]

When he died, the *Sentimental Journey* had been published, and he was writing a romance which he said was most comic.[50] He had asked only seven days more of life to finish it.

> Poor Tristrams [this is Mrs. Montagu speaking, and the word "poor" is charity] last performance was the best, his senti-mental journey would not have misbecome a young Ensign. I cannot say it was suitable to his serious profession. I used to talk in this severe manner to him, and he would shed pene-tent tears, which seem'd to shew he erred from levity, not malice. . . .[51]

The condescension of a bluestocking is credible; the tears of a jester are suspect. But didn't Sterne actually weep on this or that petty occasion? * The question is irrelevant. Tears are treacherous things, and the nations that most bravely withhold them are the most prone to sentimentality. We know something about the mind of Sterne, and can safely doubt that he saturated the paper on his desk; the people who saw him remembered him as a gay man, coarse of conversation, and with a great appetite for fame. If he did some-

---

* In raising a glass of beer, I have sometimes dropped a few beads of cold water on this manuscript. The ink is blurred. Tear-stains, as every scholar knows.

times weep in company, he may or may not have had what those who are frightened of tears would call sufficient reason. It's a poor actor who cannot make himself cry by twisting a button of his jacket; and tears have bubbled from strong men at the marriage of two notes of music, or a dying fall of words.

But what are we overlooking? Was Sterne deeply moved by nothing? Was he never truly in love?

All things are possible.

Were there no knots in the belly of his soul? He must—says the man of science—he must have been miserable down there without knowing it. And surely he was constant to something besides a jest.

Shall we be profound?

No.

5

The Second Inn: A Sentimental Journey

THE MAN WHO LOOKS morally down his nose at Sterne is invited, before he passes judgment, to explore the cesspool of his own self-interest. The egotistical affectations of Sterne were as harmless and open as the grimaces of a clown; he changed costume before the eyes of his audience; he frankly enjoyed himself as the good Lord made him, and the Lord had not made him serious.

Frivolity was his mainspring. The *Journal to Eliza* was a mere affair of flimflam gallantry; if it fails to tick, that is because passion does not go by main force of trifling—and so much the worse for it. In the two works by which Sterne is known, his frivolity and he together exist as art. *Tristram Shandy* is the fruit of all that he found laugh-at-able in his way; now comes the final fling, the *Sentimental Journey*, in which he takes a family of jokes from *Tristram Shandy* (modish ideas which by other people were courted and pursued in earnest) and writes a book about them—not as a satirist, but as a jester capitalising on things of the moment, and having his fun.

The young fellow [Yorick's new valet, La Fleur], said the landlord, is beloved by all the town, and there is scarce a corner in Montriul, where the want of him will not be felt: he has but one misfortune in the world, continued he, "He is always in love." I am heartily glad of it, said I; 'twill save me the trouble every night of putting my breeches under my head. In saying this, I was making not so much La Fleur's eloge, as my own, having been in love, with one princess or other, al-

[80]

most all my life, and I hope I shall go on so till I die, being firmly persuaded, that if ever I do a mean action, it must be in some interval betwixt one passion and another: whilst this interregnum lasts, I always perceive my heart locked up, I can scarce find in it to give Misery a sixpence; and therefore I always get out of it as fast as I can, and the moment I am re-kindled, I am all generosity and good-will again; and would do anything in the world, either for or with any one, if they will but satisfy me there is no sin in it.

But in saying this, sure I am commending the passion, not myself.[1]

It was a pleasant conceit to make philandering the parent of philanthropy; heat expands the heart, by anybody's law of physics, but the effects—we are glad to learn—are likely to be subtle: un-der these combined influences he would do anything in the world, not only for, but with anyone—provided there was no sin in it. Who was thinking of the possibility of sin? And now notice the undulant grace with which he slithers away into another corner: he is commending the passion, not himself. Sterne's is a slippery wit, and the reader must be quick to catch every word as it glides by him. Did the word "misfortune," for example, pass unrecognized, riding the circus-horse of Love?

Critics and scholars are as apt to bolt their literary meals as are those boorish common readers for whom, in matters of taste, they legislate. How else than by gross feeding can a man fail to notice the humorous flavor of the very first course in the *Sentimen-tal Journey?* The values of the finer feelings as opposed to and in-effably beyond the reach of a selfish, dry philosophy of materialism —such lights and shades are going to be played with, to the edifica-tion of all who are capable of enjoying the show. This our author tells us in the only way it ought to be told—for in trying to translate him I have distorted the effect of his art, and run the risk of con-fining to a set program a temper that swerves and glances at will. Let this be a warning.

On the first and second pages he complains of the *droit d'aubaine* with that combination of melodrama, irony, and humorous anti-climax which often distinguishes but never defines his wit.

Ungenerous! to seize upon the wreck of an unwary passenger, whom your subjects had beckon'd to their coast. By heaven! SIRE, it is not well done; and much does it grieve me, 'tis the monarch of a people so civilized and courteous, and so renowned for sentiment and fine feelings, that I have to reason with.

But I have scarce set foot in your dominions. . . .[2]

The Sentimental Traveler keeps his mind open and his heart warm in order to enjoy the amazing effects that good, unvarnished Nature has on both body and spirit.

When I had finished my dinner, and drank the King of France's health, to satisfy my mind that I bore him no spleen, but, on the contrary, high honour for the humanity of his temper, I rose up an inch taller for the accommodation.

No, said I, the Bourbon is by no means a cruel race: they may be misled like other people; but there is a mildness in their blood. As I acknowledged this, I felt a suffusion of a finer kind upon my cheek—more warm and friendly to man than what Burgundy (at least of two livres a bottle, which was such as I had been drinking) could have produced.

The suggestion of a rivalry between superior sentiments and superior wines may be invidious. We must shake it out of our heads.

Just God! said I, kicking my portmanteau aside, what is there in this world's goods which should sharpen our spirits, and make so many kind-hearted brethren of us fall out so cruelly as we do by the way?

When man is at peace with man, how much lighter than a feather is the heaviest of metals in his hand! he pulls out his purse, and holding it airily and uncompress'd, looks round him, *as if* [italics mine] he sought for an object to share it with. In doing this, I felt every vessel in my frame dilate, the arteries beat all chearily together, and every power which sustained life, performed it with so little friction, that 'twould have confounded the most *physical precieuse* in France: with all her materialism, she could scarce have called me a machine.

[82]

I'm confident, said I to myself, I should have overset her creed.

The accession of that idea carried Nature, at that time, as high as she could go: I was at peace with the world before, and this finish'd the treaty with myself.[3]

Yorick does not allow this mood of spiritual self-congratulation to last either in him or in us (though from Thackeray down to the present our tutors have whipped us into believing that Sterne, when he is not being dirty, spends his skill in imploring us, with a stupid lack of humor, to admire the tenderness of his heart). A moment later a poor monk comes in to ask alms for his convent. "No man," says Yorick, "cares to have his virtues the sport of contingencies." The monk makes a fine pathetic figure, and tells his story with such grace—

I was bewitch'd not to have been struck with it———
A better reason was, I had predetermined not to give him a single sous.[4]

When he finally melts, it is to make a liberal gesture in front of a pretty woman.

That is enough to begin with—enough for anyone who in reading a book has the least desire to see what the author is setting before him.

As the monk retires, the heart of Yorick is properly smitten for so bad a prelude to his travels. He says that he would have given twenty livres for an advocate—a sufficient comment on the initial stinginess. In order to stay out of sight of the Franciscan, he climbs into a single-seat chaise (the Desobligeant) that he finds in "tolerable harmony" with his feelings, and writes the preface to his journey. He writes it now—as in supposing a man to pull out his purse, he expected us to realise that he himself had at that moment pulled out his own; an event takes place while Sterne records it, and here we read over his shoulder as the movement of his pen, in its disquisition on the various kinds of travelers, makes the Desobligeant see-saw disturbingly. He gets out of the chaise, as he entered it, by merging authorship with life:

But there is no nation under heaven—and GOD is my record (before whose tribunal I must one day come and give an account of this work) that I do not speak it vauntingly—but there is no nation under heaven abounding with more variety of learning, where the sciences may be more fitly woo'd, or more surely won, than here; where art is encouraged, and will soon rise high; where Nature (take her altogether) has so little to answer for, and, to close all, where there is more wit and variety of character to feed the mind with. Where then, my dear countrymen, are you going?

We are only looking at this chaise, said they. Your most obedient servant, said I, skipping out of it, and pulling off my hat. We were wondering, said one of them, who, I found, was an *inquisitive Traveller*, what could occasion its motion. 'Twas the agitation, said I coolly, of writing a preface. I never heard, said the other, who was a *simple Traveller*, of a preface wrote in a *Desobligeant*. It would have been better, said I, in a Vis *a* Vis.[5]

Though while seated in it Yorick announced to us that he was to be known as one of the race of Sentimental Travelers, the Desobligeant has been a machine of farce and whimsy. The serious-minded are easily led astray, however, and Thackeray, taking him at his word, assumes that what follows is meant to be pathetic.

I had wrote myself pretty well out of conceit with the *Desobligeant*; and Mons. Dessein speaking of it, with a shrug, as if it would no way suit me, it immediately struck my fancy that it belong'd to some *innocent Traveller*, who, on his return home, had left it to Mons. Dessein's honour to make the most of. Four months had elapsed since it had finished its career of Europe in the corner of Mons. Dessein's coach-yard; and having sallied out from thence but a vampt-up business at the first, though it had been twice taken to pieces on Mount Sennis, it had not profited much by its adventures—but by none so little as the standing so many months unpitied in the corner of Mons. Dessein's coach-yard. Much indeed was not to be said for it—but something might—and when a few words will rescue misery out of her distress, I hate the man who can be a churl of them.

Here is where Thackeray interrupts us:

Does anybody believe that this is a real Sentiment? that this luxury of generosity, this gallant rescue of Misery—out of an old cab, is genuine feeling? It is as genuine as the virtuous oratory of Joseph Surface. . . .[6]

H. D. Traill for once disagrees, though without following up any of the implications of his reading of the passage. It is gratifying to hear him ask if this is not "an obvious piece of mock pathetic." [7] The incident should be brought to its full close.

Now was I the master of this hotel, said I, laying the point of my fore-finger on Mons. Dessein's breast, I would inevitably make a point of getting rid of this unfortunate *Desobligeant*; it stands swinging reproaches at you every time you pass by it.

Mon Dieu! said Mons. Dessein; I have no interest. Except the interest, said I, which men of a certain turn of mind take, Mons. Dessein, in their own sensations: I'm persuaded, to a man who feels for others as well as for himself, every rainy night, disguise it as you will, must cast a damp upon your spirits. You suffer, Mons. Dessein, as much as the machine.

I have always observed, when there is as much *sour* as *sweet* in a compliment, that an Englishman is eternally at a loss within himself, whether to take it or let it alone: a Frenchman never is: Mons. Dessein made me a bow.

C'est bien vrai, said he. But in this case I should only exchange one disquietude for another, and with loss: figure to yourself, my dear Sir, that in giving you a chaise which would fall to pieces before you had got half way to Paris—figure to yourself how much I should suffer, in giving an ill impression of myself to a man of honour, and lying at the mercy, as I must do, *d'un homme d'esprit*.

The dose was made up exactly after my own prescription; so I could not help taking it, and returning Mons. Dessein his bow, without more casuistry we walk'd together towards his Remise, to take a view of his magazine of chaises.[8]

It is not like Yorick to point out the difference between himself and an *innocent* traveler, but his newly-invented generic term slips in to make its pun with so simple an air, that the betrayal does no harm to Yorick and caresses the sleepy reader.

Guile is not interesting unless it is all innocence. Left alone with a lady (the one for whose benefit he reverses his uncharitableness towards the monk) he feels, and promises faithfully to record, certain temptations. They are to be described, he says, with the same simplicity with which he felt them. And we find that he was tempted to be of service to the owner of an "interesting" face; the simplicity resides in his easy reduction of sentimental benevolence to plain but polite love-making.

He is still holding the lady's hand when the monk comes in again. The men exchange snuff-boxes, and Good Nature hovers above them all on the wings of a flirtation. Then the monk takes his leave, and to end the chapter the bird swoops down and carries us into the future, where there is a grave—for Yorick has a sense of propriety—for us to drop a tear upon.

> I feel a damp upon my spirits, as I am going to add, that in my last return through Calais, upon inquiring after Father Lorenzo, I heard he had been dead near three months, and was buried, not in his convent, but, according to his desire, in a little cemetery belonging to it, about two leagues off. I had a strong desire to see where they had laid him—when upon pulling out his little horn box, as I sat by his grave, and plucking up a nettle or two at the head of it, which had no business to grow there, they all struck together so forcibly upon my affections, that I burst into a flood of tears. But I am as weak as a woman; and I beg the world not to smile, but pity me.[9]

He has plucked up nettles and been weak as a woman before, but never with such casual-seeming art. The cemetery was "about two" leagues off, and he is there in a moment; the nettles even are kept at a minimum; and last of all, our Yorick himself begs the world not to smile. The next words begin a new chapter of truly Shandean continuity.

> I had never quitted the lady's hand all this time; and had held it so long, that it would have been indecent to have let it go, without first pressing it to my lips. . . .

"At that crisis" the Inquisitive Traveler and the Simple Traveler happen by, and, taking Yorick and the lady to be "at least" man and wife, ask them if they are going to Paris. Yorick is for Paris, and the lady for Amiens. The officious intruders offer advice, and only the monk's horn snuff-box, talisman of good nature, saves them from an explosion.

> I was going to return a thousand thanks for the intelligence, *that Amiens was in the road to Paris;* but upon pulling out my poor monk's little horn box to take a pinch of snuff, I made them a quiet bow, and wished them a good passage to Dover. They left us alone.[10]

The Sentimental Traveler was on the brink of forgetting himself. Unfortunately the two must part, anyhow; but their roads cross again, and Yorick is able to look forward to their sitting together in a chaise—close enough for him to hear her story. "With what a moral delight will it crown my journey, in sharing in the sickening incidents of a tale of misery told to me by such a sufferer!" [11] But the soup would be thin if Yorick did not thicken it by sharing the reader's distrust of his motives. The thought of Eliza strikes him (he had promised to immortalise her in his new work). Why this is infidelity!

> Eternal fountain of happiness! said I, kneeling down upon the ground, be thou my witness, and every pure spirit which tastes it, be my witness also, That I would not travel to Brussels, unless Eliza went along with me, did the road lead me towards heaven.
> In transports of this kind, the heart, in spite of the understanding, will always say too much.[12]

[87]

Even the reader who had never before met with Yorick and his apostrophes all kneeling, or who had never seen what precedes this passage, might be expected not to pass the sly reference to "transports" without noticing it.

Transports, whether they are accepted by the devil (as Yorick once said they would be), or by the reading public (as Yorick knew very well they were), are among the wilder outward indulgences of feeling. Yorick was also cognizant of one of the subtlest signs of emotionalism, which spread like a root underground throughout the whole area of sensibility and pushed upwards to flower in the noon of the next day after his. He only glanced at the subject over his shoulder, but, like it or not, here is Sterne laughing prophetically at Shelley the Sentimentalist.

> But there is nothing unmix'd in this world; and some of the gravest of our divines have carried it so far as to affirm, that enjoyment itself was attended even with a sigh, and that the greatest *they knew of* terminated *in a general way*, in little better than a convulsion.[13]

Usually a sigh is given its full value for the length of the sentence that contains it. Having forgotten that the two countries were at war, Yorick has come to France without a passport and so is threatened with the Bastille. Here is a chance for an essay on captivity, the cause of untold numbers of sighs and groans. He begins by philosophising the evil away.

> And as for the Bastile; the terror is in the word. Make the most of it you can, said I to myself, the Bastile is but another word for a tower, and a tower is but another word for a house you can't get out of. Mercy on the gouty! for they are in it twice a year—but with nine livres a day, and pen and ink and paper and patience, albeit a man can't get out, he may do very well within, at least for a month or six weeks; at the end of which, if he is a harmless fellow, his innocence appears, and he comes out a better and wiser man than he went in.[14]

A humorist will turn this smug serenity upside down. Yorick is "interrupted in the hey-day" of his soliloquy by the reiterated "I can't get out" of the Captive Starling. Like a true humanitarian he attempts to set it free, but he cannot open the cage.

> Mechanical as the notes were, yet so true in tune to nature were they chaunted, that in one moment they overthrew all my systematic reasonings upon the Bastile; and I heavily walk'd up stairs, unsaying every word I had said in going down them.[15]

It is a Shandean custom to discourse of serious matters while going up or down stairs. Since he is now going up, Yorick gives himself an unacknowledged boost with a phrase or two borrowed from Sermon X: "Consider slavery,—what it is,—how bitter a draught, and how many millions have been made to drink it. . . ."[16]

> Disguise thyself as thou wilt, still, Slavery! said I, still thou art a bitter draught! and though thousands in all ages have been made to drink of thee, thou art no less bitter on that account.

Now a stage direction is slipped in so that we may see the comedian bow to the other side of him. Any other writer would have begun his new apostrophe with Liberty's name.

> 'Tis thou, thrice sweet and gracious goddess, addressing myself to LIBERTY, whom all in public or in private worship, whose taste is grateful, and ever will be so, till NATURE herself shall change; no *tint* of words can spot thy snowy mantle, or chymic power turn thy sceptre into iron; with thee to smile upon him as he eats his crust, the swain is happier than his monarch, from whose court thou art exiled.

And now Heaven is addressed, and we are exactly informed of the awkward position in which the suppliant kneels.

> Gracious heaven! cried I, kneeling down upon the last step but one in my ascent, grant me but health, thou great Bestower of it, and give me but this fair goddess as my companion, and shower down thy mitres, if it seems good unto

[89]

thy divine providence, upon those heads which are aching for
them.*

The complaint of the Captive still pursues him. In his room he
leans his head on his hand and prepares to gorge the sensibilities
by meditating on "the miseries of confinement." At first he has
some difficulty in focussing his imagination; slavery in general is
affecting enough, he finds, but the multiplicity of its images distracts him.

> I took a single captive, and having first shut him up in his
> dungeon, I then look'd through the twilight of his grated door
> to take his picture.

Much more satisfactory. He prepares a livid color and brushes
the canvas with it. When he discovers that one aspect of the prisoner makes his heart bleed, he is "forced to go on with another
part of the portrait"—which he makes even more horrid. There
are chains and groans. "He gave a deep sigh; I saw the iron enter
into his soul." It is too much.† Yorick bursts into tears and at
the same instant decides that he must get that passport. "I'll go
directly, said I, myself to Monsieur le Duc de Choiseul." [17]
Finding nothing on his way that is worthy of record, Yorick fills
in with the history of the pathetic starling which "became" the
subject of the preceding chapter. The bird had been taught to say,
"I can't get out" by the little English groom who caught it—a boy

* A *Sentimental Journey*, p. 77. Sometimes the humor of Sterne is not merely
ignored, it is abolished. In Enfield's *Speaker*, under *"Descriptive Pieces—Liberty and Slavery"* we find: "It is thou, LIBERTY, thrice sweet and gracious
goddess, whom . . ." and "Gracious Heaven! grant me but health . . ."—
William Enfield, LL.D., *The Speaker*: or, Miscellaneous Pieces, selected from
the best English writers, and disposed under proper heads, with a view to facili-
tate the improvement of youth in reading and speaking—To which 'is prefixed
an essay on Elocution (London, 1774). Many editions on into the nineteenth
century.
† It is too much for Traill, who has been pondering techniques of The
Novel, rather than enjoying the show. "Regarded as a substantive appeal to
the emotions," he says, "it is open to the criticisms which apply to most other
of Sterne's too deliberate attempts at the pathetic. The details of the picture
are too much insisted on, and there is too much of self-consciousness in the
artist."—*Sterne*, p. 165. A jester on the other hand (or does the name Yorick
mean nothing?) is all self-consciousness; he himself is the entertainment.

who had a sense of humor. For those who are still holding their handkerchiefs in their hands I quote the most affecting part of the tale.

In my return from Italy I brought him with me to the country in whose language he had learn'd his notes, and telling the story of him to Lord A——, Lord A begg'd the bird of me. In a week Lord A gave him to Lord B——; Lord B made a present of him to Lord C——; and Lord C's gentleman sold him to Lord D's for a shilling. Lord D gave him to Lord E——, and so on—half round the alphabet. From that rank he pass'd into the lower house, and pass'd the hands of as many commoners. But as all these wanted to *get in*, and my bird wanted to *get out*, he had almost as little store set by him in London as in Paris.

It is impossible but many of my readers must have heard of him; and if any by mere chance have ever seen him, I beg leave to inform them, that that bird was my bird or some vile copy set up to represent him.

I have nothing farther to add upon him, but that from that time to this, I have borne this poor starling as the crest to my arms.

And let the herald's officers twist his neck about if they dare.[18]

After this long preparation, built up of Bastilles and bird cages and their prisoners, and climaxed by a hurried journey to Versailles and lectures to himself on diplomatic behavior—he finds that the Duke is too busy to see him. "I think there is a fatality in it: I seldom go to the place I set out for." *

Sterne cannot easily be said to have left out of his book anything that ought to be found in the course of a sentimental journey. Most readers will be satisfied with its inclusiveness. Yet only one or two episodes appear to have been fitted in more as makeweights than as fuel for the light of humor, and these—the story of the Sword of Rennes, and the bucolic Supper and Grace—are followed each by a chapter of full-blown comedy. They are not, be

* Was a tear shed over a starling? *Cf.* Sidney Lee, p. xiii above.

it noticed, on the critics' list of damnable sentimentalities; they are minute conventionalisms, potboilers, but pleasant and deftly written—and, as Yorick says, "It would be wicked to withhold a pleasure from the good." Even so, in the chapter on the Grace there is a glint of satiric utility:

> . . . all his life long he had made it a rule, after supper was over, to call out his family to dance and rejoice; believing, he said, that a cheerful and contented mind was the best sort of thanks to Heaven that an illiterate peasant could pay.
> Or a learned prelate either, said I.[19]

It is enough if the unspoiled peasantry appear once in the book. Yorick has the mind of a townsman, and, like the jesters and clowns of Shakespeare, sparks his wit on sophistication. Nature, he says, is shy; the practised Sentimental Traveler goes up a dark entry in quest of her, and sometimes finds "a single short scene of hers, worth all the sentiments of a dozen French plays compounded together."[20] If the sentiments in his fragments of drama are far from disinterested, that must be the fault of nature. In general they are refinements of sensuality that creep up on the sentimental abstractions and tickle them under their platonic robes. This is what makes his critics leap into the air and denounce him for a dirty dog; he has touched them in their tenderest spot. "There is not a page in Sterne's writing," says Thackeray,[21] "but has something that were better away, a latent corruption—a hint as of an impure presence." And Coleridge: "Sterne cannot be too severely censured for . . . using the best dispositions of our nature as the panders and condiments for the basest."[22] And Leslie Stephen: "One often closes it [the *Sentimental Journey*] with a mixture of disgust and regret. The disgust needs no explanation; the regret is caused by our feeling that something has been missed which ought to have been in the writer's power."[23] It isn't that Sterne cannot keep things on a level of spirituality, but that he is amused by reminding people that nothing was ever on such a level to begin with.

The result is not always farce. His interest in the suffering soul of the lady at Dessein's depended on the propinquity of her body; the incident died imperceptibly away on the winds of literary nonsense. No more delicate comedy has appeared in English than that of the Grisset and her pulse; full as it is of undertones, it makes the lightest of impressions on the auditor, and having sounded its key at the outset it continues flawless to the end. "There are worse occupations in this world," says Yorick, "than feeling a woman's pulse." There are worse occupations than writing such a paragraph as this one:

> I had counted twenty pulsations, and was going on fast towards the fortieth, when her husband coming unexpected from a back parlour into the shop, put me a little out of my reckoning. 'Twas nobody but her husband, she said, so I began a fresh score. Monsieur is so good, quoth she, as he pass'd by us, as to give himself the trouble of feeling my pulse. The husband took off his hat, and making me a bow, said, I did him too much honour; and having said that, he put on his hat and walk'd out.[24]

Farce itself in this book is exquisitely managed. The Sentimental Traveler says that he has by long habit perfected himself in the interpretation of "turns of looks and limbs," and in the putting them into words. For example—and the sentimental reader complacently awaits the sentimental illustration.

> I was going one evening to Martini's concert at Milan, and was just entering the door of the hall, when the Marquisina di F—— was coming out in a sort of a hurry, she was almost upon me before I saw her; so I gave a spring to one side to let her pass. She had done the same, and on the same side too: so we ran our heads together: she instantly got to the other side to get out: I was just as unfortunate as she had been; for I had sprung to that side, and opposed her passage again. We both flew together to the other side, and then back, and so on. It was ridiculous. We both blush'd intolerably. So I did at last the thing I should have done at first: I stood stock still, and the Marquisina had no more difficulty. I had no power to go into the room, till I had made her so much reparation as to wait and follow her with my eye to the end of the passage.

She look'd back twice, and walk'd along it rather sideways, as if she would make room for any one coming up stairs to pass her. No, said I; that's a vile translation: the Marquisina has a right to the best apology I can make her; and that opening is left for me to do it in. So I ran and begg'd pardon for the embarrassment I had given her, saying it was my intention to have made her way. She answered, she was guided by the same intention towards me; so we reciprocally thank'd each other. She was at the top of the stairs; and seeing no *chichesbee* near her, I begg'd to hand her to her coach; so we went down the stairs, stopping at every third step to talk of the concert and the adventure. Upon my word, Madame, said I, when I had handed her in, I made six different efforts to let you go out. And I made six efforts, replied she, to let you enter. I wish to heaven you would make a seventh, said I. With all my heart, said she, making room. Life is too short to be long about the forms of it, so I instantly stepp'd in, and she carried me home with her. And what became of the concert, St. Cecilia, who, I suppose, was at it, knows more than I.

I will only add, that the connection which arose out of the translation, gave me more pleasure than any one I had the honour to make in Italy.[25]

The open heart, like the open (however immoderately winking) eye, is deferred to throughout. Charity itself is given three full curtsies at least, but all of them with something in the mind besides a virtue.* In one instance, not only does Yorick take a well-advertised satisfaction in sprinkling a parsimonious largesse, but he allows extraneous thoughts to stay in their natural place among his motives.

> I had then but three sous left: so I gave one, simply *pour l'amour de Dieu*, which was the footing on which it was begg'd. The poor woman had a dislocated hip; so it could not be well upon any other motive.[26]

* Thackeray, without really looking, accuses Sterne of setting down "in immense figures on the credit side of his account the sous he gives away to the Montreuil beggars."

Some may call this really unpleasant. Perhaps it is. But it is not the avowal of a sentimentalist. There is a frankness about a jester that is sadly to seek among the more respectable figures of literature; keep your eyes open, and you always know where you are with him. Often enough he will set your compass for you—as Sterne does in the course of his set-piece on the unfortunate Chevalier de St. Louis, who was so neatly got up, and whose wares were so cleanly covered with damask, "that one might have bought his *patés* of him, as much from appetite as sentiment." [27] Or he may lay his irony out on a table, so that a chapter called "The Act of Charity" becomes an affair of flattery, or blackmail by implication, and you can't think how to rename it.[28]

Sterne makes an odd sort of connoisseur of the feelings. He wrote the *Sentimental Journey* as a lark, but he threw the whole heart into his bubbling pot. A jester doesn't care so long as he amuses himself, but a declared satirist would do less damage. If Fielding had taken it into his head to do a *Sentimental Journey*, sentimentality would have been brilliantly mocked, but the heart would have been reset on a throne of tender truth. Not so in Sterne, where the merest good will is teased as if it were an extreme absurdity of the humanitarian vogue—and finally, like everything else, left in mid air by the juggler when a new toy of wit or whimsy sails into his sight.

At the opera a large German stands in front of a dwarf and unfeelingly ignores the latter's attempts to get a view of the stage.

> I was just then taking a pinch of snuff out of my monk's little horn box. And how would thy meek and courteous spirit, my dear monk! so temper'd to *bear and forbear!* how sweetly would it have lent an ear to this poor soul's complaint!
>
> The old French officer, seeing me lift up my eyes with an emotion, as I made the apostrophe, took the liberty to ask me what was the matter. I told him the story in three words, and added, how inhuman it was.

The histrionic exaggeration is familiar, and so is the trick—that never fails to surprise and delight—of letting one of his characters overhear him as he talks to the reader. Having made clear the in-

[95]

humanity of the German's behavior, Yorick has the pleasure of
seeing a sentinel place the dwarf in front of his tormentor. So
much for that; Yorick wastes no time in burning incense to the
kindly heart, though he makes yet one more reference to the invaluable smugness that is the reward of those concerned in a good
action.

> This is noble! said I, clapping my hands together. And yet
> you would not permit this, said the old officer, in England.
> In England, dear Sir, said I, *we sit all at our ease.*
> The old French officer would have set me at unity with
> myself, in case I had been at variance, by saying it was a *bon
> mot,* and as a *bon mot* is always worth something at Paris,
> he offered me a pinch of snuff.

And now he is free to go on with something scatological at the expense of a "poor Abbé," of the French, and of his dozing readers.

> Good God! said I, turning pale with astonishment, is it
> possible, that a people so smit with sentiment should at the
> same time be so unclean, and so unlike themselves! Quelle
> grossiereté! added I.[29]

Did the reader doze on? A humorist waits for no man, and Sterne's
French officer is soon explaining that there is a balance of good
and bad everywhere, and that travel teaches mutual toleration,
and that mutual toleration ("concluded he, making me a bow")
teaches us mutual love.

> The old French officer delivered this with an air of such
> candour and good sense, as coincided with my first favourable
> impressions of his character. I thought I loved the man; but I
> fear I mistook the object—'twas my own way of thinking—
> the difference was, I could not have expressed it half so
> well.

To the critics, who are responsible for the preservation of literature, this is known as congratulating oneself on one's own feelings.
The dissertation ends with an apostrophe on the innocent candour

of a Frenchwoman in stopping the coach in which Yorick and she were riding. Sterne's diction here may fruitfully be compared with that of any other apostrophe he ever wrote.

> Grieve not, gentle traveller, to let Madame de Rambouliet p-ss on. And, ye fair mystic nymphs! go each one *pluck your rose*, and scatter them in your path, for Madame de Rambouliet did no more. I handed Madame de Rambouliet out of the coach; and had I been the priest of the chaste CASTALIA, I could not have served at her fountain with a more respectful decorum.[30]

He unquestionably had a knack.

During a contest of wit and *sous-entendu* with the Count de B——, Yorick says to the reader, "I have something within me which cannot bear the shock of the least indecent insinuation." [31] The remark would be good enough even if it did not include—in surroundings so brightly illuminated that the reader who does not wish to see must shut the book—one of his favorite phrases, the sentimental "something within me," the *je ne sais quoi* of all unearthly creatures. But the book already had been written in little, many pages before, when Yorick impudently made his farce of feeling rise out of a common obscenity. La Fleur had been having trouble with the Bidet, which first refused to go by a dead ass and then threw his rider. The valet comforted himself with profanity in a rising scale; and Yorick elaborately explained to us that in the French language there are three "terms of exclamation," used like the positive, comparative, and superlative. The weakest is *Le Diable!* The second, considerably stronger, is *Peste!*

> And for the third——
> But here my heart is wrung with pity and fellow-feeling, when I reflect what miseries must have been their lot, and how bitterly so refined a people must have smarted, to have forced upon them the use of it.
> Grant me, O ye powers which touch the tongue with eloquence in distress!—whatever is my *cast*, grant me but decent words to exclaim in, and I will give my nature way.

But as these were not to be had in France, I resolved to take every evil just as it befel me, without any exclamation at all.[32]

A moment later we have begun the famous chapter on the Dead Ass—the same dead ass that was the cause of so much extravagant nonsense on the page before. How do Sterne's critics pop out of one mood and plunge into another with such reckless impropriety? And how, after a highly inventive (if not the ultimate) mockery of Pity and Fellow-Feeling, do they manage to bleed a tear or explode with fury if the tear does not come?

The story is one more whimsical exercise in the vein announced by the title of the book. The reader should certainly be aware, by the time he meets the Dead Ass, of some of Sterne's humorous devices; and so the word "apostrophe," if nothing else, ought to make him sit up. If he has come upon the story with no previous introduction to Sterne, he ought to be put on his guard by the announcement that Sterne is going to bring Cervantes up to date and at the same time outdo him.

> And this, said he, putting the remains of a crust into his wallet, and this should have been thy portion, said he, hadst thou been alive to have shared it with me. I thought by the accent, it had been an apostrophe to his child; but 'twas to his ass, and to the very ass we had seen dead in the road, which had occasioned La Fleur's misadventure. The man seemed to lament it much; and it instantly brought into my mind Sancho's lamentation for his; but he did it with more true touches of nature.

Those who think that language should hint at the intention of the man who uses it, and awaken in the hearer something of the spirit in which a thing is said, will read this tale with as much pleasure as Sterne had in writing it. They will admire, for instance, the words "mourner" and "little arrangement" in the paragraph that follows.

> The mourner was sitting upon a stone-bench at the door, with the ass's pannel and its bridle on one side, which he took up from time to time, then laid them down, look'd at them

and shook his head. He then took his crust of bread out of his wallet again, as if to eat it; held it some time in his hand, then laid it upon the bit of his ass's bridle, looked wistfully at the little arrangement he had made, and then gave a sigh.*

At home in Franconia the mourner had lost two of his sons, and when his third fell ill he vowed, "if Heaven would not take him from him also, he would go in gratitude to St. Iago in Spain." The jester continues with fine restraint:

> He said, Heaven had accepted the conditions, and that he had set out from his cottage with this poor creature, who had been a patient partner of his journey, that it had eat the same bread with him all the way, and was unto him as a friend.

"The ass, he said, he was assured loved him"; and he went on to say that as they journeyed back over the Pyrenees they had become separated for three days,

> during which time the ass had sought him as much as he had sought the ass, and that they had neither scarce eat or drank till they met.[33]

"Of course," murmurs the sentimental reader. "At that touching reunion both ass and man talked over their adventures." But alas! we find only to lose again. The combined weight of the rider and his afflictions was too much for the ass, and "shortened the poor creature's days."

> Shame on the world! said I to myself; did we love each other, as this poor soul but loved his ass, 'twould be something.

Yorick and his reader are now in a mood that requires a slow and meditative rhythm. But the jester has behaved himself long

* A *Sentimental Journey*, p. 42. Traill manages to get through this scene with the assumption intact that it is supposed to be un-selfconscious. "Is it true," he asks, "that in any country, among any people however emotional, grief—real, unaffected, un-selfconscious grief—ever did or ever could display itself by such a trick as that of laying a piece of bread on the bit of a dead ass's bridle?"—*Sterne*, pp. 161–2. Clearly not every man can appreciate so tasteful an act of homage; but is Traill, in his avidity for realism, recommending an exhibition of quite unbridled sorrow?

enough; he is tired of asserting his presence by a mere quiet working of his eyebrows. We are all in for a rough ride.

The concern which the poor fellow's story threw me into required some attention: the postillion paid not the least to it, but set off upon the *pavé* in a full gallop.

The thirstiest soul in the most sandy desert of Arabia [34] could not have wished more for a cup of cold water, than mine did for grave and quiet movements; and I should have had an high opinion of the postillion, had he but stolen off with me in something like a pensive pace. On the contrary, as the mourner finished his lamentation, the fellow gave an unfeeling lash to each of his beasts, and set off clattering like a thousand devils.

I called to him as loud as I could, for heaven's sake to go slower, and the louder I called, the more unmercifully he galloped. The duce take him and his galloping too, said I, he'll go on tearing my nerves to pieces till he has worked me into a foolish passion, and then he'll go slow, that I may enjoy the sweets of it.[35]

When the gallop is over we find that the tale of the Dead Ass and all our precious sensibilities have been jounced out somewhere along the way.

The postillion managed the point to a miracle: by the time he had got to the foot of a steep hill about half a league from Nampont, he had put me out of temper with him and then with myself, for being so.

My case then required a different treatment; and a good rattling gallop would have been of real service to me.

Then, prithee, get on; get on, my good lad, said I.

The postillion pointed to the hill. I then tried to return back to the story of the poor German and his ass, but I had broke the clue and could no more get into it again, than the postillion could into a trot.

The duce go, said I, with it all! Here am I sitting as candidly disposed to make the best of the worst, as ever wight was, and all runs counter.

There is one sweet lenitive at least for evils, which Nature holds out to us: so I took it kindly at her hands, and fell asleep; and the first word which roused me was *Amiens*.

Bless me! said I, rubbing my eyes; this is the very town where my poor lady is to come.[36]

Here we ought, perhaps, to listen to some authoritative objections. Says Traill:

The whole incident, in short, is one of those examples of the deliberate-pathetic with which Sterne's highly natural art had least, and his highly artificial nature most, to do. He is never so unsuccessful as when, after formally announcing as it were that he means to be touching, he proceeds to select his subject, to marshal his characters, to group his accessories, and with painful and painfully apparent elaboration to work up his scene to the weeping point. There is . . . no spontaneity of treatment about this "Dead Ass" episode.[37]

He apparently sees nothing absurd in weeping over a dead ass; the thing simply isn't done right. The desire to write Sterne's book for him, and the vision of an announcement "as it were": these are at the root of Traill's discomfort. Mr. George Sampson, having made the same assumption that Sterne "means to be touching," is equally disappointed:

When the "spot-lights" are manipulated with design so palpable as in the death of Le Fevre or the story of the dead ass, the author goes far to defeat his own purpose; for he at once calls in question his own artistic sincerity.[38]

(*Le Fevre*, by the way, is spelled by Sterne *Le Fever*. It is possible that the impulse behind the almost universal habit of correcting Sterne's orthography does not content itself with that one kind of distortion.) In Leslie Stephen, disappointment turns to contempt. "It seems to me," he says, "that, in trying to heighten the effect, he has just crossed the dangerous limit which divides sympathetic from derisive laughter." [39] Only Thackeray is able to transform his frustration into creative delight:

At Nampont [he] gets out of the chaise and whimpers over that famous dead donkey, for which any sentimentalist may cry who will. It is agreeably and skilfully done—that dead jackass: like M. de Soubise's cook on the campaign, Sterne dresses it, and serves it up quite tender and with a very piquante sauce. But tears and fine feelings, and a white pocket-handkerchief, and a funeral sermon, and horses and feathers, and a procession of mutes, and a hearse with a dead donkey inside! Psha, mountebank! I'll not give thee one penny more for that trick, donkey and all! [40]

The dead donkey is, of course, a famous one. The traditional way of looking at it was established without effort. According to Horace Walpole, Sterne "had too much sentiment to have any feeling. A dead ass was more important to him than a living mother." [41] The *mot* was good enough to remember, in a general way if not word for word; and we find Byron writing in his Journal, in 1813, "Ah, I am as bad as that dog Sterne, who preferred whining over 'a dead ass to relieving a living mother.'" By 1831 Walpole has fallen out and Byron has dropped behind, but the ass goes marching on. It is written in *Noctes Ambrosianae:*

A puny, sickly sensibility there is, which is averse frae all the realities of life; and Byron or somebody else spoke well when he said that Sterne preferred whining over a dead ass to relieving a living mother! But wha was Sterne? As shallow a sentimentalist as ever grat—or rather tried to greet.

The word is spread over the world by Taine, in his history of our literature. "Then there is Sterne," he says, "the refined and sickly rascal who, in the midst of his buffooneries and oddities, stops to weep over an ass that he encounters or a prisoner that he imagines."

The reaction of most critics to Sterne is curious. It is somewhat as if, after reading "The Walrus and the Carpenter" or Swift's "Last week I saw a woman flayed, and you will hardly believe how much it altered her person for the worse," a man were to inscribe in the margin: *Unconvincing*. Perhaps the world would

[102]

hardly go round if it were not for the friction between one mind and another; we listen with our ears turned inward, and look into another's eyes to see ourselves. As for humor, in its infinitely variable forms it dies hourly before it flowers, blasted by the frost between utterance and apprehension.

Those who assume that Sterne is trying to do a job of pathos also assume that he weeps over the picture. This may be legitimate as a secondary assumption, but as a statement of fact it is not unassailable. In the interests of accuracy, then, we may note that in spite of Sidney Lee (see p. xiii), Sterne has not represented himself as shedding over a dead ass even a solitary tear. Regrettable but true; altogether he has played us a mean trick.

Yet this is nothing. On one occasion he cheats the audience outrageously. Yorick finds, on a piece of waste paper which La Fleur had used in bringing him some butter, a story written "in the old French of Rabelais's time." With great pains he makes it out and translates it for us—a jolly tale of a Notary who goes out to walk on a windy night, and is suddenly called in to write from dictation the history of a dying man, "old, infirm, and broken-hearted." * We are got ready, we are set on the edge of our chairs, we await an orgy of the finer feelings.

> It is a story, Monsieur le Notaire, said the gentleman, which will rouse up every affection in nature; it will kill the humane, and touch the heart of cruelty herself with pity——
>
> The Notary was inflamed with a desire to begin, and put his pen a third time into his inkhorn, and the old gentleman turning a little more towards the Notary, began to dictate his story in these words——
>
> And where is the rest of it, La Fleur? said I; he just then entered the room.

Yorick begins a new chapter.

> When La Fleur came up close to the table, and was made to comprehend what I wanted, he told me there were only

* Like Yorick in *Tristram Shandy?* (See p. 6.) One winces for Traill and those who follow him in sympathetically requiring to know what caused the breakage.

[103]

two other sheets of it, which he had wrapt round the stalks of a *bouquet* to keep it together, which he had presented to the *demoiselle* upon the *boulevards*. Then prithee, La Fleur, said I, step back to her to the Count de B——'s hotel, and *see if thou canst get it*. There is no doubt of it, said La Fleur, and away he flew.

In a very little time the poor fellow came back quite out of breath, with deeper marks of disappointment in his looks than could arise from the simple irreparability of the fragment. *Juste ciel!* in less than two minutes that the poor fellow had taken his last tender farewel of her, his faithless mistress had given his *gage d'amour* to one of the Count's footmen, the footman to a young sempstress, and the sempstress to a fidler with my fragment at the end of it. Our misfortunes were involved together: I gave a sigh, and La Fleur echo'd it back again to my ear.

How perfidious! cried La Fleur. How unlucky! said I.

I should not have been mortified, Monsieur, quoth La Fleur, if she had lost it. Nor I, La Fleur, said I, had I found it.

Whether I did or no will be seen hereafter.*

So he leaves it, utterly lost. No wonder Sterne is disliked by so many good people.

The best they can do is cling to the neck of Maria. For she appears again, the same lunatic of *Tristram Shandy*; and the merriment is as good as ever, but the play is more stylised, more restrained—a pretty parody rather than a farce. Yorick goes in search of this interesting friend of Mr. Shandy's.

The story he had told of that disorder'd maid affected me not a little in the reading; [42] but when I got within the neighborhood where she lived, it returned so strong into my mind, that I could not resist an impulse which prompted me to go

---

* A *Sentimental Journey*, pp. 112, 113. Walter Sichel, nothing if not willing, finds this tale poetical and more "convincing" than "the stock pathos of the monk at Calais, or the twice-told whimpers over the dead ass by the wayside." *Sterne*, a Study (London, 1910), pp. 194–5.

half a league out of the road, to the village where her parents dwelt, to inquire after her.

'Tis going, I own, like the knight of the Woeful Countenance, in quest of melancholy adventures; but I know not how it is, but I am never so perfectly conscious of the existence of a soul within me, as when I am entangled with them.[43]

It is all here—the "something within me," the confutation of materialism, the languid beating of the pulse in consonance with the mood; but no wild postillion gallops away with us. The scene is sustained. The almost ceramic details are few, and colored by the pastoral suggestion of green and white; there is fragility in the very air, as if it came through a drawing-room window.

When we had got within half a league of Moulines, at a little opening in the road leading to a thicket, I discovered poor Maria sitting under a poplar. She was sitting with her elbow in her lap, and her head leaning on one side within her hand; a small brook ran at the foot of the tree.

You could pick it all up and put it on a tea-tray.

In velvet slippers the jester circles his figurine, and his voice is as small as her pipe.

Her goat had been as faithless as her lover: and she had got a little dog in lieu of him. . . .[44]
She had . . . strayed as far as Rome, and walk'd round St. Peter's once and return'd back. . . .[45]

When it is time for tears, Yorick plays a silent game with a handkerchief, a reminder of Maria's endless alternate glances at her goat and at Tristram Shandy. He does not ask if he should go on, for the point being made has answered his question.

I sat down close by her; and Maria let me wipe them away as they fell, with my handkerchief. I then steep'd it in my own, and then in hers, and then in mine, and then I wip'd hers again, and as I did it, I felt such undescribable emotions within

> me, as I am sure could not be accounted for from any com-
> binations of matter and motion.
>
> I am positive I have a soul; nor can all the books with which
> materialists have pestered the world ever convince me to the
> contrary.*

A parson need not have wandered so far afield in order to pluck
this bright assurance; but at last Yorick has given his grateful audience "a riot of the affections." The ensuing pages swarm with apostrophes, not to Castalia this time, but to Sensibility and to Nature
and to HEAVEN, the "great, great SENSORIUM of the world." [46] And
having made Heaven quiver in sympathy like a mass of human
flesh, he has finished with the soul—from now on a deliciously
pulsing substance.

The book ends, in a reflected glow of the same stylistic extravagance, with a sensual joke—The Case of Delicacy. The problem
is an intriguing one: how to go to bed by necessity in the same
room with a strange lady protected by her youthful maid. It offers
a hundred chances to juggle the absurd diction of heart and soul.
After an apostrophic preface, Sterne confines himself to the action;
and though this takes precedence over contemplation, there are
plenty of references to weights hanging upon delicate spirits, to
nice sensations, and the like. Does he feel?

> The lady had scarce warm'd herself five minutes at the fire,
> before she began to turn her head back, and give a look at
> the beds; and the oftener she cast her eyes that way, the more
> they return'd perplex'd. I felt for her—and for myself; for in a
> few minutes, what by her looks, and the case itself, I found
> myself as much embarrassed as it was possible the lady could
> be herself.[47]

Does he mention religion?

* A *Sentimental Journey*, p. 122. "The temptation to laugh," says Traill
(*Sterne*, p. 158), "becomes almost irresistible." Why not yield? Even so good
a critic as Traill is not always a careful reader: "We proceed, however, to the
account of Maria's wanderings to Rome and back . . ." Not to put a finer point
upon it than Sterne did, there is a difference between wandering to Rome and
back, and—straying as far as Rome, and walking round St. Peter's once, and
returning back.

. . . the articles were settled finally betwixt us, and stipulated for in form and manner of a treaty of peace—and I believe with as much religion and good faith on both sides, as in any treaty which has yet had the honour of being handed down to posterity.[48]

Does he affirm his innocence?

There was but one point forgot in this treaty, and that was the manner in which the lady and myself should be obliged to undress and get to bed. There was one way of doing it, and that I leave to the reader to devise; protesting as I do, that if it is not the most delicate in nature, 'tis the fault of his own imagination—against which this is not my first complaint.[49]

Has he neglected the torments or the consolations of the tremulous fancy?

. . . the two beds were both of them so very small, as to cut us off from every idea of the lady and the maid lying together; which in either of them, could it have been feasible, my lying beside them, though a thing not to be wish'd, yet there was nothing in it so terrible which the imagination might not have pass'd over without torment.

As for the little room within, it offer'd little or no consolation to us. . . .[50]

But the situation does not overwhelm them. The lady has some life in her, and the Fille de Chambre is inquisitive, and our delicate author survives, as we knew he would, to the final aposiopesis.

6

Conclusion—a Mere Preface

PREACHER AND JESTER ALIKE, we are all men of letters. When Yorick tumbled through the church door and skipped into the world with *Tristram Shandy* in his pockets, he had come into his inheritance of the whole vocabulary of the race. What he chose to do with it revealed to himself and to others what he was and what he wanted to be. Man's territory is a wide one; and though a jester be as large as life, he can gallop over only a few acres of it astride his stick. It was part of the genius and limitation of Sterne that he saw best what was within a few feet of his nose; if he knew no dimensions in depth, he was master of the subtleties of the façade; his only interior was a hearthside one, and the firelight made a merry place, miles from the dark corners of the room.

There are men who shy away from the superficial as there are men who shrink from the profound; and there are some to whom one or the other is simply unknown. Both are a fabric of words. All of us cover the hide of the brute with the clothes of art; those precious jewels, our complicated high-toned states of mind, we owe to literature. The savage cannot yawn without pedantry, and civilised man, naked for bed or for war, is plastered with the leaves of an infinite book. Some of those leaves, Sterne, like millions who wear them, could not read; but since he could not read the rest without laughing, he gathered all together and kept the unknown with the known as a wardrobe of words for his amusement. The difference between Sterne and other shallow men is that he made comic art of what is called a disability. He is a master, and of a species that is unwanted. The giants of the world become its oxen; the small slippery fellows are feared like the first in Eden, and are hunted down. In impishly putting on any face that for the moment pleases him, Sterne shivers the worm-eaten timbers of a world whose lies are serious.

Double meanings are occasionally useful; they may allow a jester to save his life and an unsmiling listener to keep his sanity. The organic irreverence of Sterne has goaded the graver members of his audience to such prodigies of labored misapprehension, that they have not only conceived but borne him anew, a black sheep, but somehow in the image of themselves and their special cravings. It may be that none but the young, the unlicked and callow, the pure in heart, the irretrievably debauched, can afford to look at him as he is. Who knows?

He is not a nice man, but he is worth reading all the same. He is not cruel, unless it is cruelty to make a joke of kindness; and the joke is often a good one. Though he cares for little beyond himself, he makes fun of all self-indulgence; and though he is always an actor, he is no pretender. He is the humorist of appearances; what men choose to call realities can neither be liked nor laughed at until they have been cut away from their roots of feeling. Saintsbury said that Sterne does not laugh but sniggers; what he does is rather to keep himself in a state of crackling amusement—kindling nonsense, and malice, and the humors of his workmanship, with the spark of impropriety. His literary technique is no more artfully unconventional than his wit. But his sense of humor is not unique. In his use of the equivoque he is close kin to Shakespeare, most of whose jollier puns—lucky for him—are no longer understood. Sterne lived with language as all poets do, and the poet who has no obscenity in him is an impostor.

To the sentimentalist of yesterday, today, and tomorrow, as to the plain honest man, something is sacred; to Sterne everything is words, the immaterial substance out of which appear the clothes, the rattle, and the handspring of a jester. The proof of his craft in words lies open to us, phrase after phrase; and the small world he made gesticulates and bows and fibs and listens at keyholes, all to the motion of his hand. The jester sets the pace and every word follows. Only look at his style, the fleet shadow of his mind. Try to put your finger on it. It slides along swiftly, easily, to right and to left—not zigzag, but in a continuous stream, it curls back upon itself like smoke, and away.

The show goes on between the covers of a book. It is a long time since the man died. God rest his bones, but there is little doubt that the dust they have become is still dancing.

Notes

Foreword

1. See also Hall-Stevenson's pseudo-Shandean "Sentimental Dialogue between two Souls, in the palpable Bodies of an English Lady of Quality, and an Irish Gentleman." (*Works*, London, 1795, II, 241.) Refined banter is made an accompaniment to unrefined goings-on.

2. Rufus Putney, "The Evolution of *A Sentimental Journey*," *Philological Quarterly*, XIX (Oct. 1940).
3. Carl August Behmer, *Laurence Sterne und C. M. Wieland, Forschungen zur neueren Litteraturgeschichte* (Munich, 1899), IX.

Chapter 1

1. *Memoirs of a Sentimentalist*, reprinted in *European Magazine*, X (July), 1786.
2. *The Lounger*, No. 20, 1785.
3. *Letters of Laurence Sterne*, ed. Lewis Perry Curtis (Oxford, 1935), pp. 12–15.
4. *Ibid.*, p. 256.
5. *The Letters of Horace Walpole*, ed. Mrs. Paget Toynbee (Oxford, 1903), IV, 370.
6. *Correspondence of Richard Hurd and William Mason* (Cambridge, 1932), p. 53.
7. Diderot, *Lettres à Sophie Volland*, ed. André Babelon (Paris, 1930), II, 194–95.
8. Voltaire, *Dictionnaire philosophique*. Article *Conscience*.
9. Francis Brown Barton, *Etude sur l'influence de Laurence Sterne en France au dix-huitième siècle* (Paris, 1911), p. 9.
10. *Ibid.*, pp. 21, 37.
11. H. W. Thayer, *Laurence Sterne in Germany* (New York, 1905).
12. John Ferriar, M.D., *Illustrations of Sterne* (London, 1812), I, 18.

13. *Ibid.*, II, 53.
14. W. M. Thackeray, *The English Humorists.*
15. H. D. Traill, *Sterne*, English Men of Letters Series (New York, 1882).

16. Leslie Stephen, *Hours in a Library* (London, 1907), IV, 70.
17. Cyril Connolly, *The Condemned Playground* (New York, 1946), p. 21.

Chapter 2

T stands for *Tristram Shandy;* references are to book and chapter respectively. The text (ed. Saintsbury) is that in Everyman's Library.

1. T—V, 32.
2. T—IX, 12.
3. T—IX, 26.
4. T—VII, 34.
5. T—III, 20.
6. T—III, 34.
7. T—I, 18.
8. T—VII, 29.
9. T—VIII, 22.
10. T—VIII, 20.
11. T—VII, 31.
12. T—IV, 1.
13. T—V, 15.
14. T—III, 29.
15. T—I, 3.
16. T—V, 3.
17. T—V, 7–10.
18. T—IX, 5.
19. T—III, 29.
20. T—VII, 40.
21. T—I, 12.
22. T—V, 2.
23. T—V, 3.

24. T—V, 6.
25. T—V, 6.
26. T—V, 7–10.
27. T—V, 11.
28. T—VI, 5.
29. T—VI, 6.
30. T—VI, 6.
31. T—VI, 7.
32. T—VI, 8.
33. T—VI, 8.
34. T—VI, 10.
35. T—VI, 10.
36. *History of the English Novel*, iv, 260 ff.
37. *Op. cit.*, p. 166.
38. T—III, 4.
39. T—IX, 6, 7.
40. T—IX, 6.
41. T—VII, 32.
42. T—VII, 32.
43. T—IX, 24.
44. T—IX, 24.

Chapter 3

L stands for *Letters of Laurence Sterne*, ed. Lewis Perry Curtis (Oxford, 1935).

1. Lewis Perry Curtis, *The Politicks of Laurence Sterne* (Oxford, 1929), p. 133.

2. L—84.
3. L—74.
4. L—75 ff.

5. L—78.
6. L—86.
7. L—88.
8. L—115.
9. L—120.
10. L—231.
11. L—87, n. 4.
12. L—432.
13. *Monthly Review*, XXIV, 106.
14. *Ibid.* XXVI, 31–41.
15. *Ibid.* XXXII, 138–9.
16. L—150.
17. L—186.
18. L—189.
19. L—234.
20. L—282 ff.
21. L—286.
22. L—287.
23. L—300.
24. L—301.
25. L—370.
26. L—400.
27. L—392.
28. L—401.
29. L—402.
30. L—404.
31. L—401.
32. P. 231.
33. Wilbur L. Cross, *The Life and Times of Laurence Sterne* (3rd ed., New Haven, 1929), p. 56.
34. P. 104.
35. *Sermons*, II, 97, in *The Complete Works and Life of Laurence Sterne*, with an Introduction by Wilbur L. Cross (The Clonmel Society, 1904), Vol. V.
36. *Ibid.* II, 98.
37. L—134.
38. *Correspondence of Thomas Gray*, ed. Paget Toynbee and Leonard Whibley (Oxford, 1935), II, 681.
39. *Sermons*, I, 19.
40. *Ibid.*, I, 32–3.
41. *Ibid.*, I, 47.
42. *Ibid.*, I, 47.
43. *Judges*, xix, 1–3.
44. *Sermons*, I, 286.
45. *Ibid.*, I, 327.
46. *Ibid.*, II, 123.
47. *Ibid.*, I, 327.
48. *Ibid.*, I, 325.
49. *Ibid.*, I, 331.
50. L—247.
51. See p. 100, n. 34.
52. L—117.
53. L—120.
54. L—138.
55. L—151.
56. L—223.
57. L—157.
58. L—162.
59. L—154.
60. L—163.
61. L—159, n. 10.
62. L—242.
63. L—213.
64. *Bibliothek der deutschen Klassiker*, VI, 652.

Chapter 4

1. L—146.
2. L—407.
3. L—10 ff.
4. L—16.
5. L—17.
6. L—18.
7. L—124.
8. Arnold Wright and William

Lutley Sclater, *Sterne's Eliza*
(London, 1922), p. 137.
9. L—398.
10. L—446.
11. L—307.
12. L—301.
13. L—347.
14. L—290.
15. L—372.
16. L—402.
17. L—256.
18. L—viii.
19. L—81.
20. L—82.
21. L—83.
22. L—96.
23. L—102.
24. L—104.
25. *Sterne's Eliza*, p. 61.
26. *Ibid.*, p. 138.
27. L—298.
28. L—304.
29. T—VIII, 11.
30. L—379.
31. L—321.
32. L—315.
33. L—317.
34. L—327.
35. L—338.
36. L—349.
37. L—384.
38. L—329.
39. L—342.
40. L—353.
41. L—360.
42. L—382.
43. L—360.
44. L—399.
45. L—311.
46. L—391.
47. L—406.
48. L—386.
49. L—394.
50. L—415.
51. *Mrs. Montagu*, ed. Blunt
(London [1923]), I, 197.

Chapter 5

S stands for *A Sentimental Journey*, Everyman's Library edition.
1. S—36.
2. S—3.
3. S—4.
4. S—7.
5. S—13.
6. *The English Humorists.*
7. *Sterne,* English Men of Letters Series (1882), p. 157.
8. S—14.
9. S—22.
10. S—23.
11. S—46.
12. S—47.
13. S—93.
14. S—75.
15. S—76.
16. Sermons, I, 169.
17. S—78.
18. S—79.
19. S—128.
20. S—114.
21. *Op. cit.*
22. *Literary Remains.*
23. *Hours in a Library* (London, 1907), IV, 70.
24. S—57.
25. S—61.
26. S—39.
27. S—84.
28. S—114.
29. S—65, 66.
30. S—67.

31. S—89.
32. S—41.
33. S—43.
34. See p. 52, n. 51.
35. S—44.
36. S—45.
37. *Op. cit.*, p. 162.
38. *The Concise Cambridge History of English Literature*, p. 510.
39. *Op. cit.*, IV, 88.
40. *Op. cit.*

41. *Walpoliana*, ed. John Pinkerton (London, 1799), pp. 133–34.
42. See p. 31.
43. S—121.
44. S—122.
45. S—123.
46. S—125.
47. S—130.
48. S—132.
49. S—133.
50. S—131.